TALKS TO GIRLS

Talks to Girls

Classic Teachings on Virtues & Values

ELEANOR A. HUNTER

AMERICAN
Tract Society

NAVPRESS

BRINGING TRUTH TO LIFE
NavPress Publishing Group
P.O. Box 35001, Colorado Springs, Colorado 80935

The Navigators is an international Christian organiza-
tion. Our mission is to reach, disciple, and equip
people to know Christ and to make Him known
through successive generations. We envision multi-
tudes of diverse people in the United States and every
other nation who have a passionate love for Christ,
live a lifestyle of sharing Christ's love, and multiply
spiritual laborers among those without Christ.

NavPress is the publishing ministry of The Navigators. NavPress publications help believers learn bibli-
cal truth and apply what they learn to their lives and
ministries. Our mission is to stimulate spiritual formation among our readers.

(Originally published as *Talks to Girls* by Eleanor A.
Hunter, © copyright 1891 American Tract Society,
New York. This edition by permission.)

Cover illustration: Wood River Gallery

All Scripture quotations in this publication are taken
from the *King James Version* (KJV).

Printed in the United States of America

1 2 3 4 5 6 7 8 9 10 11 12 13 14 15 / 00 99 98 97 96

Contents

I wish and I wish that the Spring would go faster,
Nor long Summer bide so late;
And that I could grow on like the fox-glove and aster,
For some things are ill to wait.

⋅⊸══◉══⊷⋅

I wait for the day when dear hearts shall discover,
While dear hands are laid on my head,
The child is a woman, the book may close over,
For all the lessons are said

—JEAN INGELOW

Preface

While circumstances and society have changed significantly within the past 100 years, right and wrong remain the same. But in a society where many no longer recognize the value of truth, honesty, and living upright and godly lives, it can be difficult to teach our children their necessity.

Originally published in 1891, *Talks to Girls* gives you a unique tool for teaching your children classic virtues and values. Each short essay on a different subject gives you a glimpse into the past, while teaching a timeless lesson suitable for any age.

Whether you read each chapter aloud as a family or encourage your children to read them alone, you'll be delighted with these charming lessons and stories from the past.

Questions for discussion have been added to the end of every chapter, giving you the opportunity to discuss each topic as a family. Few changes have been made to the text itself, with the exception of footnotes added to clarify the author's intention and selected words changed where necessary.

Talks to Girls was originally published by the American Tract Society. Founded in 1825, the American Tract Society was at one time the largest publisher of both Christian and secular titles in the world. During the 1800s and early 1900s, the society published works by many well-known authors and theologians, including John Bunyan and Jonathan Edwards. The American Tract Society also published biographies, devotionals, reference works, books of theology, and children's books.

In the 1940s, they stopped publishing books and focused exclusively on tracts (pocket-sized pamphlets). Most of their current tracts emphasize evangelism for all occasions on a variety of contemporary subjects and social issues. American Tract Society is one of the largest producers of gospel tracts in the world today, publishing between twenty to thirty million each year. A free full-color tract catalog is available by calling (800)54-TRACT or (972)276-9408. For further information about the background and current ministry of the American Tract Society write P.O. Box 462008, Garland, TX 75046 or visit their web site at http://www.goshen.net/AmericanTractSociety

NavPress and the American Tract Society have an exclusive publishing relationship, in which NavPress will republish selected works from the American Tract Society book archives that address classic spirituality, family, and Puritan theology.

Talks to Girls

An Ideal Womanhood

A perfect woman, nobly planned
To warn, to comfort, and command,
And yet a spirit still, and bright
With something of an angel-light.

WORDSWORTH

THERE ARE VERY FEW GIRLS WHO DO NOT ASPIRE TO BECOME lovely women, who do not feel, at least at times, the beauty of a sweet, a noble, and an exalted life. And yet all women are not noble and good and lovely. Sometimes, when they have every opportunity apparently to become all that they might be and all that they should be, they fall short and fail to develop fully the noble capabilities of their nature; while those to whom circumstances have not been so kind often make the truer women. Sometimes the reason of this is because girls do not always understand the best way in which to develop and cultivate character. They are too young

11

to have what an artist would call "a just estimate of values." Things which are really important they miss, and things which are but trifles they suppose to be valuable. This is true of lessons, work, play, reading, clothes, behavior, and thoughts, too, sometimes, and in fact of everything that makes up daily life.

It is for such girls that this little series of papers is written. The one who writes them was once a girl herself, and she has not yet forgotten the puzzles, the mistakes, and the trials which belong to the years of girlhood. And so I shall talk to you about your lessons, your work and your play, your clothes and your behavior, and your faults, too, sometimes, and in fact of everything that makes up your daily life, in the hope that I may help you in your efforts to grow into true and lovely Christian women. But I cannot *do* anything for you; at best I can only *help* you a little. All the real work of character-building you must do for yourself.

The rarest advantages, the noblest friends, the finest spiritual atmosphere are all nothing to a girl if she does not appreciate them and lay hold upon them and lift herself by them up to a higher plane.

But if she honestly tries to reflect in her own life the beauty of the Savior she will surely succeed, for no such effort ever escapes the watchful eye of our heavenly Father, and He is sure to give to every earnest soul exactly the help it needs in order to grow like Him. So in whatever condition a girl may be born— high or low, rich or poor—if she will, she may grow to be just such a woman as the poet thought of when he wrought the four lovely lines at the head of this chapter. She may become *a perfect woman*.

⇥ For Further Thought ⇤

1. Think of a young woman you admire. Why do you admire her? (*Hint:* Look beyond appearance for your answer.)
2. You'll meet a few people in life who inspire you to want to be like them. But there is only one person who ever lived on this earth who could be called perfect. Who is that person? (See 1 Peter 2:21-22.)

Girls and Mothers

Sweetest Mercy, your mother taught you
All uses and cares that to maids belong.

INGELOW

She comforts all her mother's days,
And with her sweet, obedient ways
She makes her labors light.

INGELOW

In these days of strain and hurry, of high school and college, of music and of art, some poor girls seem to have no time in which to learn those "gracious household ways" which only a mother can teach. If Maid Marion turns her attention at all to the subject of domestic economy, she goes to cooking school, and after a term with Miss Corson or Miss Parloa she thinks she has mastered the whole science. But a cooking school, however good, is a poor substitute for a girl's own mother, as many a girl finds out when she enters a home of her own and gathers the various forces that govern the household machine into her little, inexperienced hands and tries to control them. She is a brave girl if, at the end of the first week, she does not cry for her mother to come and help her. Her mother will go, of course; but now the child has come to a spot where her mother, with all her love and experience, cannot help her greatly; she must learn for herself. She has plunged into the midst of a sea of trouble, and she must struggle out as best she can. And the saddest part of it is that Maid Marion, even if she brings plenty of sense and courage into the conflict, will never be as perfect a housekeeper as she would have been had she mastered the science little by little at her mother's side during the days of her girlhood, any more than a woman of forty can learn to speak a foreign language perfectly. She may understand its construction, but the accent, the ease of speech, will be lacking.

There is another side to the question. Girls are not likely to be closely under their mothers' wings for a very long time nowadays. They are only at home dur-

ing their training time. After that is over they either
marry or enter upon some business or profession and
take their parts in the duties of life. So these years at
home should be exceedingly precious to them. It is the
only time they will have to be closely associated with
their mothers, and they ought to take the opportunity
to learn the domestic arts, not only for their own
sakes, but for their mothers' sakes also. They will not
always be able to help their mothers. Some day that
dear form will be laid away to rest in the quiet church-
yard, and all her rich stores of household wisdom will
go with her; and then, perhaps, her daughter will wish
she had not only learned more of her, but that she had
helped her more while she was with her.

I know a family consisting of two daughters and
one son, and every summer they used to go during
vacation to a small farm in the country. During that
time the father and mother were the children's guests.
The son superintended the farm and the daughters
kept the house. They had a strong woman to help
them with the heavy work, and the rest they did themselves. They were up with the lark and they went to
bed when the sun set, and they were as busy and as
happy as the day was long. There was nothing about
practical housekeeping that they did not understand.
They knew how to wash flannels and prints and fine
clothes. They knew how to starch a shirt and to iron
it. They knew exactly how to boil a potato and to broil
a steak. They could make the sweetest and most

delicious bread, both white and brown. They knew how to take care of milk and they could make butter. They knew also how to order a household, how to arrange the various kinds of work, and to carry them on without bustle or fatigue. They learned all these things little by little during the years of their childhood, while their mother was always near them with encouragement and advice. In the wintertime the other part of their education was accomplished, and it was thorough, both in books and in music; and when they were grown they were noble women, morally, mentally, and physically, and were thoroughly trained on all sides for every duty in life.

There was never a time in the history of the world when woman was such a force, moral and intellectual, as she is now; but that which is physical must come before that which is spiritual. These bodies of ours must be well nourished and cared for before any great moral or intellectual height can be attained; and a girl of fifteen is not too young to think of these things, nor too young to think seriously of the place which she is to fill in life, and to try to fit herself for it. And if she wishes, as every true girl should, to be loving and beloved—one of those noble women whose lives, whether they are married or single, bless everyone who comes within their reach—she must learn, while she is yet in the days of her youth, to care intelligently for the home which God will one day give her.

⊰ FOR FURTHER THOUGHT ⊱

1. If your mom was unable to do anything at home for at least a month, and her job fell to you, how prepared would you be to step into her shoes? List three of your mom's (or your dad's) responsibilities at home. (*Hint:* balancing the checkbook and maintaining a budget; putting good, nutritious meals on the table every day; growing a garden or keeping the yard maintained. . . .) In which areas do you need training? What advantage would there be to learning this skill while you still live at home?

2. Why is it important to know how to take care of a home, even if you never get married or have children?

3. What is another good reason to learn how to run a home before you go away to college, career, or marriage? (Hint: Think about the mother and father in the story who took summer vacations at the farm.)

Needlecraft

So delicate with her needle.

SHAKESPEARE

THE OTHER DAY I WAS READING AN ARTICLE IN A POPULAR ladies' magazine on the subject of a wedding trousseau [a collection of clothing, etc., to be used after marriage], and the writer advised young women to buy their underwear ready-made, "for," wrote she, ". . . if nine girls out of ten make it for themselves it will not be neatly done." Can it be possible, thought I to myself, that such a sweeping assertion is true? And I began to think over the list of young girls whom I know to see how many of them have a knowledge of sewing. Alas! there are a good many who cannot make neatly the plainest garment. They do not even darn their own stockings.

"Don't scold," said Edith coaxingly, when I began to speak to her about it. "I cannot help it; I really have no time for sewing; with my lessons, my painting, my practicing, and my lectures in English literature, I hardly have time to breathe."

It is quite true, and I should not be surprised to learn any day that poor Edith had broken down with nervous prostration simply from overwork: and I am old-fashioned enough to think that much nervous wear and tear might be spared her if some of her studies were dropped and she were to spend from one-half to three-quarters of an hour a day at her needle.

The need of educating the body as well as the mind is now beginning to be realized, and in these days first-class schools, both for boys and girls, have gymnasiums; and that mental benefit which comes from mastering a handicraft is also recognized, and schools for boys which have a manual training department are in successful operation. And what is good for a boy is in this instance equally good for a girl. And to my mind, of all handicrafts, that of sewing is the most beautiful and most interesting. It not unfrequently rises to the dignity of an art.

Not long since I was examining a bit of dainty needlework—not embroidery, but a bit of delicate stitchery—and as I marked the beautiful hems and fells and seams, I thought, "Must such work as this become a lost art? With the advent of the sewing machine must such exquisite sewing as this cease to be valued? Shall we lose the art of sewing as we have those of spinning and weaving? I hope not, and I think not. There will never come a time when the needle will cease to be of value to mankind." It has been for thousands of years peculiarly the woman's implement, and it will be a sad day for this old world if she ever forgets how to wield it.

Needlework is good for a girl not only as a training for hand and eye in neatness, exactness, and thoroughness, but it is also good as a rest from mental labor. Half an hour's quiet sewing rests the brain. But aside from this, every woman recognizes the need in her daily life of that old-fashioned accomplishment called "plain sewing." No family can do without a seamstress, and a girl should not only be able to sew, but also to cut and fit any garment. She should be able to cut and fit and make a simple gown well, for when she is a woman grown, with all a woman's cares and responsibilities upon her, she may find the knowledge an inexpressible comfort to her.

Of course a schoolgirl cannot be expected to make her own wardrobe, but she may know how it should be done and she may make some of it herself; for during the long summer vacations she can profitably spare some golden hours to learn the craft of sewing without injuring her health or seriously infringing on her good times; and even during the crowded winter days she will find that she can devote many a half-hour to her needle, when it will be a benefit to her nerves and will give her a mechanical training which she could ill afford to do without, even if she should be so singularly situated in after years that she would not need to use the knowledge thus acquired during her early life.

⊰ FOR FURTHER THOUGHT ⊱

1. What does the author's advice reveal about girls when this was written?
2. Although you probably buy most of your clothes from a clothing store, do you think it would be fun

to learn to sew for yourself? What other kinds of
things can you make?

3. How does it make you feel when you make things
with your hands?

On Fancy Work

A thing of beauty is a joy for ever.

KEATS

THERE LIES IN A CERTAIN BUREAU DRAWER IN OUR HOUSE A
square of yellow canvas bordered with a tiny wreath of
pink silk roses, and in its center is worked the following remarkable stanza of poetry:

> "When Virtue decks the wrinkled brow
> And fills with life the languid eye,
> E'en then we see a heavenly glow
> Too pure for mere mortality;
> But when Youth's bloom reflects her beams,
> All pure from Vice's tainting blight,
> Resistless then her glory streams,
> And dazzles with angelic light."

The silks with which the design is worked are faded,
but every little "cross-stitch" is truly set, and it was the

sampler of a little girl just six years old.

My heart melts with pity when I think of that poor baby setting stitch by stitch that dreadful bit of poetry. I hope she did not mind doing the roses quite so much. But this I know, that she patiently, day by day, did her "stint," until the tedious task was done, and then this morsel of a maid was very pleased and proud — as well she might be — when her parents, her teacher, and her friends praised her patience and her industry.

This was what our grandmothers used to call "fancy work"; and as I chance to know, some of these venerable ladies who are still with us look with a good deal of contempt upon the amazing beasts, birds, and fishes worked in brightly-colored wools upon cardboard which the wee folk of today bring home from the kindergartens and exhibit so proudly.

"Such work is not durable," says Grandmamma. And she is right. Nevertheless I prefer the new way to the old for very little folks, for they learn something of the laws of form and of color and how to handle a needle, and that is enough for a baby to know. But sometimes girls who are old enough to do better things do not do much worthier work than they did in their kindergarten days. Their work is not worth preserving, for it is neither useful nor beautiful, and the work is often done in a slovenly manner. It is wrong to waste time and money so. A girl ought to exercise her conscience in her fancy work as well as in anything else.

Sometimes a girl spends too much time in making pretty things, and it is a most fascinating occupation — the beautiful colors and fabrics of the materials are a great temptation to any woman; but remember, my girls, that fancy work comes after lessons and housework and plain sewing and practicing. Fancy work should not be considered as a *work* at all, excepting by those who earn their living by it, but to the ordinary girl it should be a recreation.

Not for centuries, not since the days of the great tapestries, has ornamental needlework been brought to such perfection as today; and it is an art well worth cultivating, for there is nothing which a woman can give which will be so valued by the recipient as something which has been made by the giver's own hands. There is a value in such a gift which no other token, no matter how costly it may be, can have.

It is delightful too to beautify the home with the work of one's own hands. Be careful however to make your home truly more delightful as well as prettier by your efforts. Sometimes girls make a sad mistake in home decoration. I was going to call on some friends one afternoon when I saw their younger brother sitting on the fence. He was whistling absently to himself and looking gloomily at the checkered pattern made by the fluttering shadows of the leaves upon the path. He didn't notice my approach, and I wondered what had happened to disturb him, for he was usually so light-hearted and merry that it was a pleasure to meet him.

"Good afternoon, Tom," said I cheerfully.

"Oh!" said he, starting, "good afternoon," and touching his hat, he jumped from his perch and walked by my side to the gate. As he opened it for me he said hesitatingly, "I'll bid you good-by now. I guess I won't come any farther."

"Why," said I, surprised, "won't you come in with me? I just came for a chat with the girls, and I always like to see you too."

"No," he answered in a quiet, bitter way, "I'll not come in; but the girls will be glad to see you. They have fixed the parlor all up new, and I'm not allowed in there now. I'm only at home in the barn," and he turned away.

I called for the young ladies and entered the parlor. It had evidently been recently refinished. A rich carpet of a delicate neutral tint covered the floor, and pieces of finely carved, satin-upholstered furniture were standing here and there; beautifully draped curtains hung at the windows, bits of rare bric-a-brac were scattered about, delicate lace tidies adorned some of the chairs, while others were decorated with great bows of orange ribbon; a scarf of bolting cloth painted with an exquisite design of rose sprays and butterflies was draped across an easel, and I stood in the twilight, my eyes half-blinded from the sudden transition from light to gloom, not daring to sit down lest I should crush some delicate ornament, when Alice and Maggie came in.

"Oh, how do you do?" said they. "We are so glad to see you! Don't you think the parlor is improved? We have been teasing Papa for years to let us do it, and now it is done the dining room and sitting room look so shabby beside it that he says they may be refurbished too."

"What will you do with Tom then?" I asked. "Give him something to eat on the back steps, I suppose, and not let him come into the house at all."

"Oh Tom," they answered laughingly. "Yes, we have just been scolding him. I suppose he has told you, but really he is such a Goth we can't allow him in here at all. He is so clumsy that he is sure to crush or to mash something every time he enters the room. But," they continued, "you haven't told us what you think of the parlor. Honestly, now, doesn't it look nice?"

"Honestly, then," I answered quickly, "I would rather see the parlor just as it used to be, and with Tom in it, than to have all these beautiful things here and him out; and you will be sorry some day for having treated him so rudely."

Now Alice and Maggie were not unsisterly girls, though they were thoughtless. They loved Tom, and after a little they "made up" with him, though I do not think he ever forgot the sting which they gave him when they excluded him from the parlor, and it was some time before they could coax him to come in there again. But their ideas of art were mistaken. They had many pretty things in that room, but they were not suitable for it, and an artist will tell you that any decoration which makes a room less cheerful and comfortable is false art and in bad taste, and is not to be tolerated by intelligent people, no matter how intrinsically beautiful the article may be.

Consider well, then, when you are thinking of undertaking a new piece of fancy work, whether it will be suitable for the use to which you intend to put it. Think whether it will really please people and delight them or whether it will prove to be only a bother and an annoyance. Choose wisely, and then spare no pains to make your work as perfect as possible, and when you have finished it you will have produced something which is genuine and durable and worth having, and it will be a pleasure to you whenever you think of it, whether you keep it yourself or give it to someone who has not the time or perhaps the money to spend on such pretty things.

⇥ FOR FURTHER THOUGHT ⇤

1. Why is something you make with your hands and give as a gift often more satisfying to you and the person you give it to than something you could buy?
2. When the author spoke about the two sisters who redecorated part of their house, she said, "They had many pretty things in that room, but they were not suitable for it." Why were the pretty things not suitable?

3. There is a saying: "Beauty is its own excuse for being." What does that mean? Why is that saying not true in the story? (Hint: Who or what is more important than beauty? Why?)

———————

Girls and Brothers

And were another childhood's world my share,
I would be born a little sister there.

GEORGE ELIOT

MR. EDWARD EVERETT HALE THINKS THAT THE MOST advantageous place for a child to be born in is to be born as he was—in the middle of a large family, with three or four nice bright brothers and sisters just ahead of you, and three or four nice little brothers and sisters coming along behind. Such a situation is indeed delightful, but nevertheless I agree with George Eliot that there is nothing quite so nice as being a "little sister." I suppose that is because I was a little sister myself, for I know a lady who has five younger brothers, and she always insists that to be the eldest is really the nicest of all. And when I see her with her brothers I do not wonder that she thinks so, for they all love her so much and treat her so beautifully that it is delightful to see them together. I was quite curious to see this sister, for I chanced to know her brothers before I met her, as she was spending the winter away from home. They were always talking about her and quoting her opinions and ideas. They used to read me bits of her letters and show me specimens of her pretty needlework in the shape of presents which she had given them at different times; and though the boys were utterly different from each other, yet they would all grow enthusiastic at the mention of their sister's name. At last she was coming home, and they were delighted.

"Now we will show her to you," they cried, as if she were some rare and precious object. "You will be sure to like her; everybody does."

At last I saw this wonderful girl. She was sitting in a low chair in the library and her brothers were clustered around her like bees around a rose. She did not appear to be in any way remarkable. She was just a quiet young lady in a plain gray gown. She was not very pretty nor very stylish. She had a gentle voice, a bright smile, and a sweet, sincere expression. But I have seen far more gifted and more beautiful girls many a time whose brothers were not one-half as fond and as proud of them as this girl's brothers were of her. What was the secret of her charm? It was a very simple one. She loved them; and because she loved them she was interested in everything they said and did. She could talk metallurgy with the School of Mines boy and the peculiarities of the hardware trade

with the business boy. She was Tom's confidante in his
first love affair, and she used to listen with equal interest to Jack's accounts of the girls that he "couldn't get
on with," and Ward, the youngest, always depended
upon "sister" when he came across a particularly
tough problem in school.

She loved them all so much that she was glad to
deny herself to please them. She was always ready to
amuse them. She would stay at home or go out with
them, whichever they liked. She used to play and sing
for them, talk with them, read to them, play games
with them, and she never was rude, cross, or unkind
to them. That is a great deal to say of any girl, but that
is the kind of a girl she was—always unselfish and
bright and gentle. Not that she did not speak to them
about their faults; she did, but never in the presence
of others.

Said their mother, "I do not know how I could
have brought up my sons without their sister's help.
She had a wonderful influence over them."

It was true she did a great deal for them. They
took a great deal of her time, her patience, and her
strength, but she had her reward. It is no slight thing
to have five true lovers at your beck and call, ready to
spring at your bidding and happy to fulfill your slight-
est wish; but that is exactly what this sister had. She
never lacked an escort to concert, lecture, prayer meeting, or party, or anywhere else she chose to go. Her
brothers would go on any errand for her or carry any

package—and they were no fonder of bundles than the average boy. In short, they would do anything they could to please her, and they made her very happy by their protection, their kindness, and their care.

And if any girl who reads this has brothers who are not like these boys, I can tell her the reason why. She does not love them enough.

"Oh!" you say indignantly, "I do love Frank, but he does not care anything for me; he is so rude."

Think a minute. Do you never snub him or criticize him or make fun of him? Do you never dispute with him? Do you constantly think of little things to do that will please him? Are you gentle and sweet in all your ways with him always? If you are not, you do not love him enough, for it is in such ways that sisterly love is manifested, and I do not think the boy ever lived who could resist a kind and gentle sister. You are at least partially responsible for your brother's manners and also for his morals. If you talk and laugh loudly and are given to slang, if you are rude and indifferent in your manners, so will he be. If you do not lead a true and noble Christian life, neither will he be apt to; and what is very sad, if your standard of morals is not high, he will measure all other girls by the girl he knows best. He will think they are no better than you; and one of the worst things that can befall a boy is for him to lose his respect for the character of women; and if your brother does not revere women, you could be responsible for it.

It is not every girl who thinks seriously of these things, nor every girl who is unselfish enough to win her brother's affection; but those sisters who are loving and kind and true are more than repaid for any sacrifice they may make, for there is no blessing greater than a loving, manly brother.

⊰ FOR FURTHER THOUGHT ⊱

1. What did you think when you read about this family? How does this type of relationship compare with many brother-sister relationships today?
2. When brothers and sisters don't get along, what are the usual reasons? What do you think is the root cause of this kind of behavior?
3. Describe in your own words what love for others looks like. Now read 1 Corinthians 13 and see if your description of love matches what the Bible says.

Girls and Boys

And the streets of the city shall be full of boys and girls playing in the streets thereof.

THE BIBLE

I AM ONE OF THOSE WHO HEARTILY BELIEVE IN OUR AMERICAN way of allowing girls and boys to be friends and companions. I think it an excellent thing for both to allow them to grow up together. But as they do meet in such a free and friendly way, it puts a good deal of responsibility upon both, and it is of the girls' duty that I am writing now.

Many girls do not think much of their duty to their boy friends; they only think of the good times they can have together.

Now a girl has a great influence over a boy, and every girl should realize that fact, and she should always try to use it rightly.

Have just as much fun with your boy friends as you can. Play with them all you like. "Tag" and "Touch the Goal" are just as good for girls as for boys. But be sure in all the fun never to do one deed or say one word that shall lessen a boy's respect for you.

In these happy days it is not the style for girls to be timid and frail or to faint at nothing. The modern girl is not scared at a mouse or afraid of a toad, nor does she scream at a spider. It is now considered a fine thing for a girl to run and skate and climb, for the modern girl has strong muscles and good nerves, and I am very glad of it; but with these new ways sometimes a girl takes on a freedom of manner and a rudeness of speech that spoil it all. I know it is "only in fun"; nonetheless it lowers the moral tone of the girl who so behaves. It leaves a door ajar by which worse things may enter; and not only that, but she is liable to drag her friends down with her.

So never let a word of slang soil your lips, and keep

the gentle manners of a lady always. Take for your model the lovely lady, Elizabeth Hastings, who, in the midst of a court where she had every temptation to do otherwise, yet behaved so beautifully that she won this rare compliment from a gentleman who knew her. Said he, "Though her mien carries much more of invitation than command, to behold her is an immediate check to loose behavior, and to love her is a liberal education."

That is the way your boy friends ought to feel about you.

A girl ought to be more to her boy friends than simply someone for them to have a good time with. She ought to be a positive force for good to them; but a girl is often afraid to speak to a boy upon a serious subject for fear he will laugh at her or think her "a prig." That is a mistake. If you have a boy friend who is in danger from some bad habit, sometime, when you have a good chance, speak to him frankly and kindly upon the subject.

Girls have a great influence over a boy's religious nature. Do not be afraid to use it. It is strange how tongue-tied many of us are when we attempt to say anything about our Savior, or try to get other people to know and to love our best Friend. Many a boy might be brought into the church by the aid of a friendly word. Boys of sixteen think very seriously of these things, and it is hard if a Christian girl cannot give them a little help in the right direction. Give them a

cordial invitation to go with you to the Christian
Endeavor meeting or to prayer meeting or to praise
service, and they will be very glad to accept it.

Christ has an especial love for boys and girls. He
has told us how He used to watch them playing in the
marketplace of old Jerusalem when He lived on earth;
and the verse which I have put at the head of this
article shows what happy times they will have
together when the city which He loves so well is built
anew, in that beautiful time when all the world shall
come to know and love Him. And if Christ so loves
boys and girls, and takes such thought for their happiness, it is sad if they cannot behave, both in work
and play, so as to always have His smile and blessing,
for without that there is no value in the work, nor
pleasure in the play.

⊰ For Further Thought ⊱

1. Have you ever seen or heard the Nike slogan, "Just
   Do It!" —an advertisement for athletic shoes? Adver-
   tisements usually contain a broader meaning than
   the products they sell; they reflect our culture and
   can even influence our behavior. What would the
   girl who interpreted the Nike slogan in a positive
   way be like? What would the girl who interpreted
   the Nike slogan in a negative way be like?
2. Although most things in our society have changed
   since this story was written, some things never
   change. What behaviors did the author write about

that you still face (and sometimes struggle with) today?

3. What role does self-respect play in being a girl who influences boys in a positive way?

To Schoolgirls

Oh lift your natures up,
Embrace our aims. Work out your freedom. Girls,
Knowledge is now no more a fountain sealed;
Drink deep, until the habits of the slave,
The sins of emptiness, gossip, and spite,
And slander die. Better not be at all
Than not be noble.

TENNYSON

IT WAS ON A FRIDAY AFTERNOON OF THE FIRST WEEK OF SCHOOL that some of the girls dropped in to tell me how things were going. One was perched on the arm of my sofa, two were nestled on the rug at my feet, and two more were settled in the deep window seat, and all five had been chattering pretty steadily for about half an hour. I had been told about the new steam-heating apparatus, Florence Draper's new dress, Rachel Davis's method of pronouncing French exactly as if it were English, and mademoiselle's wrath thereat [on that account], and the fact that they could not "abide" Miss

Shawe, the new teacher of English literature and history, as well as various other items of interest. At last there came a pause in the chatter, and then Hester looked up and said, "You must think we are a silly crew, Miss Margaret, after hearing all this nonsense."

"Oh no," I answered, smiling. "I should feel much hurt if my girls stopped talking nonsense before me. I should think I must have been very rude or disagreeable if I found that you were beginning to pick and choose your topics of conversation when you are with me; for I like best to know you just as you are, without any pretense or concealment, and how can I do that unless you are just your natural selves?"

"And you think our 'natural selves' are very nonsensical, don't you?" pursued Hester.

"No," I answered. "I know that my girls very often have serious thoughts, for they tell me about them sometimes, and I am waiting just now to hear something solid on the subject of school."

"Well," spoke up Jessie Freeman candidly, "I don't know that I have any very serious thoughts to offer upon that subject."

The others laughed, for Jessie was so pretty and sweet that nobody expected much more of her than just that.

"What do you go to school for, Jessie?" I inquired.

"Well," said she, "I suppose that I ought to say that I go to learn my lessons, and, of course, I do learn them after a fashion. They are a necessary evil connected with school, but really and truly I go to school because I have such a good time there."

"And Alice," said I, continuing my investigations, "what does she go to school for, I wonder?"

"For lessons," answered Alice, promptly. "I do indeed." And her answer was quite as truthful as Jessie's had been.

"But," said I, "why do you like to learn your lessons?"

"Well," said she reflectively, "if I do a thing at all, I like to do it thoroughly, and then I must say that I like to stand first. I can't bear to have anyone get ahead of me."

"But," said I, "are those the only reasons you have for learning your lessons?"

"Why, yes," she answered wonderingly, "I believe they are."

"Alice," said I, "if you could say every irregular verb in the French language without tripping, or knew the distance of every star in our planetary system from the earth, what good would it do you?"

Five pairs of astonished eyes gazed at me solemnly as Alice answered hesitatingly, "Why, I don't know."

I looked at the rest of my audience, and none of them had an answer ready.

It seems incredible, but not one of these five girls had ever seriously thought why she went to school. People had to be educated, they knew, and they went to school because it was the usual thing to do.

"Alice," said I, "if your knowledge of the French language does not lead you to explore its beautiful literature, if you do not familiarize yourself with its moving and heroic history, delight in its poetry, and instruct yourself with its prose, your knowledge of French will do you little good. And if every night when you look up at the throbbing stars you are not impressed anew with the wonders of that heavenly host, if your heart is not lifted by the sight of that which is seen, beyond them to that which is unseen, your knowledge of astronomy will not be very beneficial; for an education which does not expand both the mental and moral faculties of the scholar fails of its object. Mr. Tennyson knows what an education ought to do for a girl," I continued, and reaching out my hand for a certain little gray and crimson volume, I read to the girls the quotation which heads this chapter.

"Don't you see, my girls," said I, when I had finished, "that when the mind is occupied with noble thoughts and beautiful ideas there is no room left for anything that is small or petty or mean."

"Ah!" said Hester dolefully, "it would be easier to learn if all teachers taught like that; but it isn't every girl who has a princess for a teacher. You just ought to see Miss Shawe."

The girls laughed, but I said, "There is just where you make a mistake. Of course a fine teacher is very helpful and inspiring; you can get on faster and do better work under such training; but if you are determined to learn you can learn with a poor teacher, or indeed with no teacher at all, and the best teacher in the world cannot make a good scholar out of a poor one. That is something the scholar must do for herself."

"But," complained Jessie, "we cannot all of us be good scholars, because some of us are not so bright as others."

"It is true," I answered, "that you cannot all be equally good at lessons, for God did not give you the same capacity. But there is one thing in which you can be equal. You can each of you be perfect in your conduct every day, and as for lessons, if you all study faithfully, you need none of you fall seriously behind. And then," I continued, "it is not only of yourselves that you have to think. No one lives to himself in this world. What you are affects every one around you, and if you do not make the very best of yourself that you can, you are missing just that much of a chance to help others. Worse still, you are dragging them down, for if you are not as good as you might be, they are not as good as they would be if they had you to help them to be better.

"It is not so very long ago that girls were denied this priceless gift of a thorough education, but now the doors of schools and colleges are open wide, and the idea of Tennyson's beautiful princess has become an accomplished fact, and the world has many noble women today who are scholarly, accomplished, keen, and alert, who understand their own powers and are able to apply them where there is most need, and they are all bent, in one way or another, on making this world a nobler and a happier place than ever it was before. And you, my girls, in a few years more will have a chance to help them if you wish; and whether you render good and efficient help depends upon the use which you make of the training time that you have now."

This was rather a long lecture for me to give my girls, but they took it so quietly and sweetly that I am in hopes it will set them to thinking more seriously than they have before of the duties and privileges of their school life, and the need that they have for a thorough preparation for the years that are lying before them.

⊰ For Further Thought ⊱

1. What was Miss Margaret's message to the girls about school?
2. Why do you go to school?
3. Look up the word *noble* in the dictionary and read through all its meanings. What meaning applies to this story? How can learning, or knowledge, make a person noble?

On Truthfulness

Above all things tell no untruthe, no, not in trifels.
The custom of yit is naughte, and let yit not satisfie yow
that for a time the hearers take it for truthe, for after,
yit will be known as yit is, to your shame.

SIR HENRY SIDNEY

JENNIE AND I WERE READING TOGETHER THE LIFE OF SIR
Philip Sidney, and we came to the passage which I
have quoted above in a quaint and beautiful letter written to Sir Philip when he was a little boy at school by
his father. When I had read to the end of the sentence
I paused.

"I wish," said I, "that I could print that sentence
in letters of gold upon the walls of every schoolroom
in the land. I wish I could tell it to every boy and girl
I know and make them feel its force."

"Why," said Jennie in a surprised way, "do you
think boys and girls are so untruthful?"

"I am sorry to say it," I answered, "but I think a
good many of them are not perfectly truthful."

"I never told a lie in my life," said Jennie proudly;
"and I know plenty of other girls who never did
either."

"I am sure, Jennie," I answered, "that if you discovered that you had made a misstatement about

anything you would at once correct it, but was it not you who gave Maggie Upjohn no less than five correct dates in her history examination, and helped her on two examples, and let her copy from your definitions beside?"

"Well," said Jennie, "yes, I did; but I don't call that anything."

"Did Mrs. Annersley know it?" I asked.

"Of course not."

"Would she have allowed Maggie's examination to pass if she had?"

"Certainly not," answered Jennie. "I see what you are aiming at, Miss Margaret. Of course I would not accept any help on my examinations, but the girls would have thought me awfully mean if I had refused to help Maggie."

"That is where a schoolgirl's code of morals is often defective," said I. "You helped Maggie to do what you knew to be wrong, and what you would not do yourself, because the girls would think you mean if you didn't. To put it in plain English, you helped Maggie to deceive your teacher, and what is that but untruthfulness? It is not always that one can trace the consequences of such a deceit, but in this case the effect is very plain. Maggie did not gain her promotion by honest work, and therefore she will not be able to keep her position in her class. Mrs. Annersley was speaking to me of her yesterday. She said that Maggie had been so idle that she was surprised at her being able to win a promotion, and that she was evidently unable to keep her new position now she had it, and she should be obliged to put her back where she was before. That will be a just punishment for Maggie, but," said I, pausing, and speaking gently, "how will the girl who helped her to commit the fraud be punished?"

"Dear me, Miss Margaret," said Jennie, "you do call things by such dreadfully plain names. I suppose now that I cannot rest till I have been to Mrs. Annersley and told her about it."

"You forget that you will be obliged to involve Maggie in your confession," said I. "'Never tell on a schoolmate' was one maxim of my code when I was a schoolgirl, and it is a rule that I still believe in."

"Mrs. Annersley never wants us to tell on each other," said Jennie quickly. "I will tell her about it, but I will not mention Maggie's name, of course. It *was* a mean thing to do," said Jennie reflectively, "a very mean thing; for Mrs. Annersley always puts us on our honor during examinations, and then trusts us perfectly. I will never do such a thing again."

Exaggeration is a very prevalent form of untruthfulness, and it is a fact that a person who long indulges in the habit becomes at last incapable of telling the truth. The moral vision becomes so blurred that one is unable to perceive the outlines of any truth clearly and present it as it is.

Pretense is only another form of untruthfulness. How many a schoolgirl pretends to be brighter and better than she really is—pretends to a genuine knowledge when she has only a smattering, pretends to qualities which she never possessed and to virtues she never practiced?

Ah, if people could realize how useless such pretenses really are; for we are always estimated at our true value in this world. We can deceive no one for long. It is only by being genuinely noble and good and true that we can win love and trust and honor in return, and such a character is not built easily or soon.

Once some One lived in this world for more than thirty years as boy and man, and one of His names was Truth. He felt every temptation that can come to boys and girls, and He resisted them all, and if we watch Him closely and try to model our lives after His, we have His promise that we shall succeed. "We shall be like Him," and there is no other way than this by which we can attain perfect truth and honor.

⊰ FOR FURTHER THOUGHT ⊱

1. What's the difference between looking at someone's test paper to get an answer and letting someone look at your test paper to get an answer?

2. What ultimately happens to someone who wins a game, receives an award, or is given an 'A' grade through deceit?

3. What is another form of untruthfulness? (*Hint:* E _ _ _ _ _ _ _ tion.) Why is this just as dangerous as a lie?

On Friendship

Henceforth I call you not servants, . . .
but I have called you friends.

JESUS

A friend in need is a friend indeed.

OLD PROVERB

THEY WERE WALKING HOME FROM SCHOOL TOGETHER AND I was strolling just behind, admiring their pretty hair, their graceful walk, and their neat, dark suits that were just the thing for school. Now and then a low, musical ripple of laughter or a fragment of excited talk floated back to me, and I was thinking what a delightful thing it is to be in perfect health, just sixteen, and strolling home from school in company with your best friend on a crisp October day, when this little bit of talk caught my attention and set me to thinking: "Yes," said Goldilocks, "that is the way she always acts. She takes a girl up and is perfectly devoted to her for a week or two, and then she turns about and cannot talk too badly about that very girl."

"I know it," answered Brown-Braids, "and she had seven intimate friends, one after the other, and all during one term."

This is the little fragment of talk I heard, and which, as I say, set me to thinking.

A schoolgirl friendship is proverbially a fickle thing; people smile at it as if it were too trifling to be considered seriously. This is unjust; for often during school years friendships are formed that last a lifetime. Nevertheless many girls would do well to think of the subject more seriously than they do.

Often the people we call our friends are really only acquaintances; we are amused by them or we may admire them, but we do not love them, and there can be no real friendship without love. That is what makes the choosing of a friend such a serious thing. One ought not to make friends lightly, and a friend once made should not be easily parted with. Do not idealize your friends. Remember that they are as liable to make mistakes and errors as you are yourself; and then, when one of them does something which you do not like, you will not be disappointed, and you will remember that she may have to forgive you for something some day. Do not be too confidential with any friend. There are affairs in every family that it is neither wise nor best to confide to anyone. So if your aunt Mary's husband is in pecuniary difficulties or if your father did reprove your brother Jim for indulging in cigars, the next time you see Fanny do not tell her all about it. Maintain a noble reticence on such subjects. Never give a confidence unless some good will be accomplished by it; but if you receive a confidence, no matter how trivial, regard it as sacred.

If a misunderstanding occurs, do not draw yourself up in proud, offended silence the next time you see Fanny, but go to her frankly and say to her, "Why did you do thus and so?" or "Why did you talk like that about me?" Very probably you will discover that Fanny never said or did anything that you could object to.

There are many tests to which even a schoolgirl's friendship may be put, and in any time of trial one friend is in honor bound to stand by another. And if sickness or trouble or disaster of any kind should visit your friend, then surely you will prove to her in every way you can how much you love and sympathize with her.

But we do not always choose our friends for ourselves. Sometimes Christ chooses them for us; and when He does we should always prove faithful to the trust. Sometimes we are thrown with people who at the first do not seem at all congenial. We do, perhaps, some impulsive but kindly deed that attaches them to us; or for some reason they seem to draw us, while we do not care half so much for them. If such a friend should come to you, you should be very careful not to chill her regard; for you may be the very one chosen to be a help and comfort to that other soul and to lift it by the inspiration of your example to higher and nobler things.

Surely we should remember that when Christ chose us for friends, it was not because we were congenial or attractive to Him or because He had any need of us. No, indeed, He made friends with us solely because He wanted to do us good; and this thought should enter into all our friendships: we should try to live so that our friendship will be a benefit to our friends.

Then, though we may have, and it is quite right that we should have, some congenial companions who are nearer and dearer to us than others, we should remember that without love we can help no one. So we should try to be friendly with all whom we know, and then when the opportunity comes we shall be able to help people as we never could if they did not love us and trust us; and if we are worthy of love and trust, we shall be rich in friends and we shall be able to be a help and comfort and a minister of happiness to many.

⊰ FOR FURTHER THOUGHT ⊱

1. Do you have a best friend? What makes her different from your other friends?
2. What's the best way to handle a misunderstanding with a best friend (or any friend)?
   a. Tell others what she did.
   b. Ignore her until she apologizes.
   c. Pick a new best friend.
   d. Talk with her about it privately.
   Did you pick 'd'? Thinking the best about your friend—one aspect of loyalty—is one of the most important qualities you can show a friend.
3. Sometimes someone picks you as a friend, but you don't feel drawn to her. Why should you treat her as well as you would the friends you pick?

To Hester About Her Looks

I want to help you to grow as beautiful
as God meant you to be when
He thought of you first.

GEORGE MACDONALD

Handsome is that handsome does.

OLD PROVERB

IT IS THE MOST NATURAL THING IN THE WORLD FOR A YOUNG
girl to wish to be beautiful. Youth and beauty seem
made to grow together, and when a young girl has a
plain face and is unhappy about it, I am always sorry
for her. So the other day when Hester said sharply in
answer to a question of mine, "No, I am not going to
Isabel's party; I hate parties, and I never want to go to
another in my life," I forgave her rude tone, for I knew
at once that something had happened to hurt her feelings severely.

"What is the matter, little girl?" said I gently.
"Seems to me you are rather young to renounce parties in that wholesale fashion."

Hester's under lip quivered a little and she did not
answer for a minute, but presently she exclaimed bit-
terly, "I don't see why God couldn't have made me
pretty, as well as Belle or Margaret. I am just the
ugliest-looking girl I know. There isn't one of them all

so homely as I am, and I don't think it is fair."

"Come here, Hessie," said I; "come and sit down by me." So she came and sat on a little footstool at my feet.

"I suppose you think I am wicked," said she, "to feel so; but nobody likes me or notices me or wants to talk to me, if I do go out. And what do you think?" she went on brokenly. "At the last church social Milly Osborne asked Harry Fletcher if he wouldn't like to be introduced to me, and he said, 'Do you mean that dreadfully plain girl who sits there back of Ethel Winslow? No, thank you. One look at her is enough for me. I don't care for a closer acquaintance.' That is just what he said, for I heard him, and I thought then I would never go anywhere again, and I never will." And Hester hid her poor little face in my lap and burst into tears.

I said nothing for a few minutes, but quietly stroked her brown head until she was herself once more. Then I said, "You are right, Hester; there has been a mistake made about your looks; but God did not make it. He meant you to be a very lovely and attractive girl, so charming that people would be drawn to you at the very first sight of your face."

"You are laughing at me," said Hester.

"No, I am not," I answered. "You might be all that I say and more, but you are frustrating all God's plans for you, and so far you are not like what He meant you to be at all. Do you know that nearly always there is a little frown upon your forehead and a little sarcastic curve upon your mouth? You have no idea how much the lines of your face are improved by a kindly expression, and when you are genuinely happy your whole countenance is transfigured; but when you look as miserable and discontented as you do today, you don't look in the least as God intended you should. It is true that your nose is not exactly classical in shape. Your mouth is large and your forehead is too high for modern ideas of beauty. But your face is capable of great beauty of expression; and if you knew how fascinating a fine expression is upon a plain face you would never worry about your irregular features again.

"But I am afraid you will find that a beautiful expression is not an easy thing to win. To possess it you must forget yourself; and how often do you do that, my Hester? You are always thinking that somebody is looking at you or whispering about you or 'making fun' of you. And how can you have a sunny look when you are a prey to such miserable suspicions? You must go to Isabel's party, my dear, and you must leave all such wretched thoughts behind you. You have one real beauty that cannot be spoiled—that of perfect health; and a healthy girl with a sunny face is always a pleasant sight. And then when you go to the party, instead of waiting to be entertained and noticed, you must try at once to please and entertain someone else. If you see someone who is shy or awkward, try at once to cultivate that one, and be your very nicest and kindest to him. Exert yourself to be pleasant to your neighbor, whoever he or she may be. Consider that person to be for the moment your special guest and be your most cordial and kind while you are near each other. If you follow this plan you will not only have a pleasant time yourself, but you will be sure to give some others a happy evening also.

"Then, my dear, remember from this time on that you cannot do one generous deed or one unselfish action, you cannot even think one noble or one gentle thought, that its traces will not be left upon your face. And by-and-by, if you fill your life with beautiful thoughts and deeds, the angel which God meant you to be will look out from your eyes, smile from your lips, speak with your voice, and everyone who knows you will say, 'What a lovely woman Hester is!'"

⊰ FOR FURTHER THOUGHT ⊱

1. Name the principle taught here. (*Hint:* Forget Y _ _ _ _ _ _ .) Give an example of what that looks like.
2. How could you apply it to your life?

To Alice About Her Clothes

> I know her but in two,
> Nor can pronounce upon it
> If one should ask me whether
> The habit, hat, and feather
> Or the frock and gypsy bonnet
> Be the neater or completer;
> For nothing can be sweeter
> Than the maiden Maud in either.

TENNYSON

ALICE DROPPED IN FOR A LITTLE CALL ON HER WAY HOME FROM school a few weeks ago. Alice is one of my girls. I am both fond and proud of her. I am always glad to see her keen, bright face appear at the library door. Alice is good at mathematics—that you can tell at a glance—and I enjoy her quick intelligence, her hatred of shams, and her absolute truthfulness; and yet Alice is not attractive to people generally. On the day of which I speak, when she came in, her jacket was half-dragged from one shoulder, her collar was twisted around under one ear, her hat was dusty, her glove was ripped, three buttons were off from her shoes, and her whole appearance was careless. This did not surprise me, however, for Alice is apt to look rather careless even when she starts off in the morning, and a day at school does not mend matters. Alice took off her hat and jacket and sat down beside me.

"It is such a bore," she began; "at half past four I must be at Miss Trim's to be fitted for my new suit. I do so dislike fussing about clothes. How some girls can spend the time they do upon dress, I cannot imagine."

And Alice flung up her chin and looked so superior to "some girls" that I smiled.

"If some girls spend too much time on dress, others may not spend enough," said I. "All ought to make it a matter of conscience."

"The Bible says it is wrong to wear handsome clothes," said Alice argumentatively.

"Does it?" said I. "Where?"

"Why," answered Alice, "the apostle Paul says it, doesn't he, in that place where he says a woman's only ornament must be a 'meek and quiet spirit.'"

"That passage is in the First Epistle of Peter," said I. "Suppose you find it and read it."

So Alice found the passage and read, "'Whose adorning let it not be the outward adorning of plaiting the hair and of wearing jewels of gold or of putting on apparel, but let it be the hidden man of the heart, in the incorruptible apparel of a meek and quiet spirit, which is in the sight of God of great price.'"

"Don't you see," said I, "that means when you depend for your charm and attractiveness upon your clothes alone, you are wrong. It is the meek and quiet spirit that will make you lovely, not garments nor ornaments, no matter how beautiful they may be. The text teaches clearly that extravagance in dress is wrong, but the apostle Peter never said that it is wrong for a woman to wear suitable and becoming clothes, nor does he say that it is wrong for her to enjoy them."

"He says it is wrong to plait one's hair, though," said Alice mischievously, giving her head a wag, which set her long braid swinging. "I am going to have mine cut off."

"Ah," said I, "when the apostle said that, he meant that it was wrong for women to spend long, precious hours in arranging their hair in the elaborate fashion which was in vogue in that day. He did not refer to a simple and beautiful arrangement of the hair. On the contrary, he probably admired beautiful hair. I am sure the apostle Paul did extremely, and I think you would do very wrong to have your hair cut. Perhaps you do not remember what a compliment the apostle Paul paid to a woman's hair once; he said it was 'her glory.' Now your hair might be glorious," said I, "but—"

I looked at Alice's head. The long braid was rather rough, though that was pardonable, as she was on her way home from school, but it was tied with a crumpled, faded bit of what had once been blue ribbon, and on the fair ripples just above her temple was a great black mark where she had wiped her pen.

Alice blushed a little. "I know it does not look very nice," said she, "but it *is* such a bother to keep it in order."

"How is Dayton doing these days?" I asked, changing the subject, for I saw she was rather embarrassed. Dayton is Alice's brother.

An anxious shade came over her face. "Day is well," she answered; "but Day is not home as much evenings as Mamma wishes him to be."

"Where does he go?" I asked.

"That is the trouble," Alice answered. "We don't always know."

"Perhaps he goes to call upon Jessie Freeman," I suggested.

"No," said Alice, smiling. "He worships her from afar."

"I wish," said I, "that you could copy Jessie Freeman's charm, and then Day would admire you, and he could worship a-near, and you would always know where he was and be sure he was safe."

Alice looked a good deal annoyed. "I must say," said she, "that I do not care to copy after Jessie Freeman. I think she is a very stupid girl."

Now I am not afraid to speak plainly to Alice, or to any of my girls, in fact, when I think it is right to do so, and they always take my "plain talks" in a very sweet spirit. So I went on now. "Alice," said I, "did you ever consider why Day admires Jessie Freeman so much? Isn't it because she always looks so dainty and fresh and sweet and always has such a pleasant smile for her friends? My child, you are your brother's keeper, and think what sorrow there will be if you are

false to your trust; and if a bright ribbon or a pretty
dress will help to keep him safe, will you not take the
trouble to wear it? Day has a very susceptible and artis-
tic temperament, and he is keenly sensitive to such
influences. If I were you I would make it a matter of
conscience for the next few years to dress as prettily as
I could, just for Day. Have your dresses of the colors
and styles that he likes, wear the ribbons he fancies,
arrange your hair in the way he prefers. You have no
idea how proud he will be of you, nor how such def-
erence to his taste will please him. Be gentle and loving to him, glad to see him when he comes in, and be
your brightest and sweetest and prettiest just for him,
and see if you cannot win him to love home and you
so well that he will never wander away from you. Of
course," I went on, "it is a sin to waste too much time
and money and thought upon clothes; but, on the
other hand, it is a Christian's duty to be always neat
and tidy; it is a Christian's duty to be attractive; and
how can anyone be attractive who is not neat and
dainty in dress?"

"I never thought of it like this," said Alice slowly.
"Don't you know that in books it is always the girl in
the plain dress that is good, and the girl with the handsome clothes that is hateful and ugly?"

"But it is not the clothes which make the difference in the girls," I answered. "It is the spirit in which
they are worn. If the girl with the poor gown bears her
cross bravely, and the girl with the pretty gown takes

her blessing sweetly, they will both be lovely girls, and both will show the influence of the Spirit of Christ in their behavior. There is no subject that a young girl needs to exercise her conscience in more than this subject of dress. And there is only one way in which she can be sure she is doing right about it. It is only when she dresses as she thinks Jesus would like to have her dress that she can be sure she is safe."

When Alice kissed me good-by that afternoon she said sweetly and gravely, "I never thought like this about my clothes before. I will not forget it; you will see that I will not."

The other evening I dropped in at Mrs. Ward's. Tired Day was lying on the sofa while Alice sang "Sweet Alice, Ben Bolt" to him. When she had finished her song she swung around on the piano stool, and I had never seen her look so fresh and sweet. Her beautiful hair was in perfect order, dainty ruffles were at her throat and wrists, and she had on a little apron of dotted mull, trimmed with lace and blue ribbons, copied after one of Jessie Freeman's, and it added a final touch to a perfect little toilet. And Alice smiled and I smiled, but neither of us spoke a word, though I was very glad to see that the little seed which I had planted had taken root and was growing so finely.

⊰ FOR FURTHER THOUGHT ⊱

1. The author puts a lot of importance on the way a girl dresses. What do you think she's saying?

a. Spend all your free time shopping at the mall.
b. "You are what you wear."
c. The way you dress and the way you carry yourself shows self-respect and respect for others.

2. What messages do magazines, television, and movies give out that encourage girls to be obsessed with the way they look?

On Talking

The ill-timed truth we might have kept,
Who knows how sharp it pierced and stung?
The word we had not sense to say,
Who knows how grandly it had rung?

EDWARD R. SILL

WHEN I WAS CONSIDERABLY YOUNGER THAN I AM NOW I USED to be very fond of a certain story whose heroine was a good little girl, out of whose mouth dropped pearls and diamonds whenever she spoke; and there was in the same story a bad little girl, out of whose mouth hopped ugly toads whenever she opened it. When I used to read this story I supposed it was a fairy tale, but since I have had more experience of life I have become convinced that it is true, for I have met both sorts of girls many times; only the girls themselves are quite unconscious of both the toads and the jewels.

If you knew dear Mary Gilchrist you would recognize her for one of the good little girls at once. Mary is not particularly witty or very wise, and it is not so much the things that she says as the way she says them that makes her words seem like pearls and diamonds as they drop from her gentle lips. She is such a pleasant girl. She is like a streak of sunshine or a cool breeze or an open fire or the perfume of apple blossoms. She has reminded me of all these things at different times and seasons, and the other day she made me think of a little brook. When she entered the room Agnes and Gertrude were having a disagreement, it does not matter about what.

Said Agnes to Gertrude, "Don't be so silly! You never can do it in that way if you try it until the end of time."

"I *shall* do it," answered Gertrude, doggedly, "in just that way and no other, if I should be a thousand years about it."

I felt too worn out to try to untangle the snarl, and I am sure I do not know how long they would have stayed in that deadlock if Mary Gilchrist had not laughed — not a mean laugh, but a little gurgling, rippling laugh, just like a brook running over pebbles.

"Gerty," said she, "let me show you how to do it. I want you to come out with me this afternoon; I cannot wait a thousand years." And in ten minutes the thing was done; but before she left us she had said something kind to Agnes about her music which sent her off pleasantly to her practicing, and she had told me one or two little items of news which I found interesting, and before she left the house we were all three restored to serenity by a few words from that lovely girl.

Afterward when I spoke to Agnes about it—for she was really the aggressor—she owned at once that she was in the wrong.

"But," said she in excuse, "I am not like Mary Gilchrist; it is easy enough for her to speak pleasantly; I should have to watch every word that came out of my mouth."

"One might even try to do that," I answered, "for a habit of considerate speech is worth a great effort; but I know of an easier way still. It is 'out of the abundance of the heart that the mouth speaketh,' the Bible says, and if you will only be sure that your heart is kind and true, you will have no need to watch your words; and I am sure that that is Mary Gilchrist's plan."

A true heart will miss no chance to be kind; it will be ready on the instant to say the "right" thing; and the right thing said at the right moment is often the greatest kindness that one can give to another. But the brave word withheld through cowardice, or the gentle one through indifference, has often caused a weary soul to sink in despair.

Many persons pride themselves on a habit of what they call "plain speaking," and though "the truth or silence" should always be the rule, there are many times when it is cruel not to be still; for there are many hard and bitter facts in this world which it is the truest kindness to ignore, and, if possible, to forget.

How would we feel if we were constantly reminded of our "sins, negligences, and offenses" by our heavenly Father? He does not do so. He tells us that He "blots them out, and remembers them no more against us for ever." And so, and only so, we have the courage to "try again." Surely we ought to do the same for our fellow sinners. And if any unfortunate or mortifying fact is connected in any way with the history of a friend, surely it is the height of cruelty to remind him or her of it in any way or to mention it to anyone else.

There is a great deal of talk which is trivial and worthless. I do not mean lighthearted talk that brings a hearty laugh. Blessings on that happy soul who brings a smile wherever she goes. But I refer to the large amount of time which many people spend in aimless chatter. Have you no friend who is an inspiration to you whenever you meet—who somehow lifts you above your usual level up to a higher plane and leaves you thinking of nobler things? If you analyze that person's influence upon you, you will find that it consists in power to say things that are of worth; and if you cultivate a habit of "high thinking," too, you will also have such a faculty, and you in turn will be able to help others to nobler things.

The Creator gave no greater gift to mankind than

the gift of speech, and there is none which we should guard with greater care; for with the same tongue whose noble or gentle words can give to others help and comfort and inspiration we can also speak words which will rankle like a poisoned arrow, never to be forgotten while the heart they wounded lives.

Realizing this, surely our daily petition should be in the words of the prayer of old wise King David, "Let me take heed unto my ways, that I offend not with my lips."

⇥ FOR FURTHER THOUGHT ⇤

1. Have you ever said something you wish you'd never said?
2. Why is it a good thing to think before you speak?
3. What guidelines does the Bible provide in Ephesians 4:29 for people who want to say the right things?

"Noblesse Oblige"*

The gentler-born the maiden,
the more bound, My father,
to be sweet and serviceable.

TENNYSON

WHEN BABY ROSAMOND WAS BORN PEOPLE SAID, "SHE WILL surely be a spoiled child. With so much money in the family, such a beautiful home, such a father and mother, and all that crowd of uncles, aunts, and grandparents all vying with each other how to best please her, she will certainly be spoiled; it cannot be helped."

People repeated some of this talk to Rosamond's mother, but she was not alarmed. She took her baby in her arms and kissed her, saying, "No, she shall not be spoiled, my own little girl. They talk as if all these things must necessarily be snares to trip her poor little feet instead of blessings to help her on her upward way."

So little Rosamond had a simple, happy, wholesome child-life and girlhood, and when she was fourteen years old she and her mother had a serious and beautiful talk together.

Noblesse Oblige (noh-BLESS uh-BLEEZH) literally means "nobility obligates." It's the belief that those who have wealth and privilege should help those who are less fortunate.

"My child," said her mother, "you are now old enough to see for yourself that you have far more delights and blessings than many girls of your age. You have this beautiful home and Papa and me, and so many friends to love you; your clothes and your food, all of the best and finest, are provided for you without any thought or care of your own. You have the wisest of teachers to instruct you. You have everything that can help you to grow to be a good and noble woman. All children do not have such blessings. Some, no older than you, are obliged to earn their own living, the food they eat, the clothes they wear. Others live at home with fathers and mothers who love them just as well as Papa and I love you; but because they have not much money, they cannot give them the advantages that we give you, and they also have to deny themselves many pleasures that you have always enjoyed. Then again, some children are sick, while you are always strong and well; sometimes they are blind or deaf or have some bad deformity, while you have a body perfect in every part. Think how much more blessed you are than they."

"Mamma," said Rosamond seriously, "why should there be such a difference? I don't think it is fair. Why cannot all children in the world have things alike?"

"Ah!" answered her mother, "that is a hard, hard question, and I cannot answer it. But one thing is sure; if people who have money would help people who have none, things would be evener. Some people do try, and more people are trying in these days than ever before. Papa and I are trying, and now you are old enough to begin to help us."

I think it was this talk that changed Rosamond from a child into a thoughtful girl. It was the first of many talks with her mother upon the same subject, and Rosamond grew up with the idea of devoting her life to others, not by retiring into any sisterhood, but living in her own home, surrounded by a world of love, and being just herself, nothing but a sweet, sunny, affectionate girl. She became an accomplished house-keeper and an excellent cook, not only that she might someday easily direct a home of her own, but also that she might be able to show her poorer friends, who had never had the time to learn such arts, how to make home comfortable. She learned how to sew and to cut and fit all kinds of garments, that she might teach others how. She studied her lessons at school with the same thought and practiced her music with the same idea; and by-and-by, when schooldays were ended and she had the management of her own fortune, she gave money too. She made friends with poor girls, and shared their sorrows and anxieties and got them to share her joys. And she learned to love and to admire many of them very much.

"They are so magnificently brave, my friends who work," she said once, with a glowing face. "They have taught me far more than I have ever taught them; and how any one can speak slightingly of them or pass them carelessly by, I do not understand. Do not"—and her face grew grave—"do not people remember that our Lord and Savior was a working man? How can anyone speak lightly of work or workers knowing that?"

Rosamond lives at home and keeps up her music and is apt to read the last new book. She helps her mother with her various cares and is her father's sunshine still. She has done nothing wonderful, nothing that any girl might not do, and yet today she is beloved in hundreds of homes where in one way or another her lovely influence is felt.

Of course, in choosing the life she has, she has made some sacrifices. She has not led altogether the life that is usual with young ladies of her class. She has had fewer parties and fewer entertainments of all kinds than some of her friends, for one cannot work as Rosamond does during the daytime and then be up half the night beside. Nevertheless she is not out of society, for she meets frequently the best and most interesting people of the day. She has sacrificed in a money way also, for she makes it a rule to give until giving means self-denial. She has her days of discouragement, when her best plans are shattered and her friends mistake her meaning or fail her altogether, and when even her own temper plays her false, for Rosamond is not yet perfect. Still, in spite of every mistake and hindrance, I think that if all who, as the Prayer Book says, "profess and call themselves Christians" would live for others in the same spirit which Rosamond does, it would not be many years before all the world would learn to know and love our Lord and Savior Jesus Christ, because people could not help but believe in Him and trust in Him when they saw His spirit constantly reflected in the shining lives of His servants all about them.

⊰ FOR FURTHER THOUGHT ⊱

1. If God blesses a person with wealth, do you think they have less to worry about in life or more? Why?
2. If a girl was going to have the same attitude as Rosamond, name some ways she would probably spend her time and money.

One of Rosamond's Friends

A princess, a washer-woman, yes, a washer-woman.
To see that all was fair and clean, to wash with water,
to cleanse and purify wherever she went,
to set disorderly things in orderly array—
this was a woman's mission.

RUSKIN

NOT EVERYONE WOULD HAVE KNOWN HER TO BE A PRINCESS by her looks. Her own brothers and sisters, though they all loved her, did not suspect it; but Rosamond, who had been reading Ruskin, found it out before she had been in the house half an hour, and she always called her "my princess" behind her back, but to her face she just called her "Molly," as the others did who knew nothing of her rank.

You see, Luly, the princess' younger sister, was in Rosamond's Sunday school class, and as she did not come to Sunday school one morning, Rosamond called the next day to ask if she had been sick. Now, as everyone knows, Monday is washing day the world over, consequently Rosamond found the princess engaged in doing the family washing. And she was doing it with a sweetness of spirit and a thoroughness of manner which would have delighted Mr. Ruskin's heart. She was not at all disturbed by Rosamond's entrance. When Luly opened the door she turned, and seeing the strange young lady, she welcomed her graciously, as a princess should.

"I am afraid I have interrupted you," said Rosamond anxiously, when she saw what was going on.

"No," answered the princess with a pretty courtesy. "The clothes are in the rinsing water, and it will not hurt them to lie. I am glad to see you. Take the rocking chair."

While she spoke she calmly untied her damp apron, unpinned the skirt of her dress, unrolled her sleeves, opened a bureau drawer and took a fresh white apron, put it on, and then sat down to entertain her guest. As she took a seat the baby scrambled over to her, pulled himself to his feet by the aid of her dress, and said imperiously, "Up, up!" The princess smiled and lifted him to her lap, but as she glanced at him she cried out in dismay.

"Oh, Luly!" she said, "he has been at the blueing-bag [used when washing clothes, to tinge with blue]. Look at him!"

It was true. The baby was most picturesquely streaked in dark blue from his top curl to his toes, and he looked more like a young tattooed South Sea Islander than a Christian baby.

But even this did not upset the princess' fine poise. "Bring some water and a cloth, Luly," said she, quietly.

The baby gurgled out a little laugh. Then Rosamond laughed. "Doesn't he look cunning!" she exclaimed.

The princess lifted pleased and grateful eyes. "Oh, ma'am," said she, "he is always cunning, no matter what he does."

At this commendation the baby was pleased to laugh again, and so they took one more laugh all around while the baby was being washed and inserted in a clean pinafore, and at last was exhibited without decorations.

"He is a lovely child," said Rosamond, with unaffected interest. "How old is he?"

"Eleven months and five days," said the princess, with proud accuracy. "He has four teeth already and two more coming, but he is not cross a bit any of the time."

"Delightful!" said Rosamond. "But," turning to Luly, "I missed my little scholar yesterday. Where was she? I was afraid she was sick."

Luly looked a little embarrassed; but the princess was not. She was old enough to know that even in the richest kingdom the exchequer [national treasury] sometimes becomes impoverished; so she explained calmly, "No, Luly was not sick, but she has been needing a new pair of shoes for some time, and Saturday I had to send her on an errand, and I told her to tread careful; and so she did, but she slipped on a piece of ice and tore the sole right off from one shoe, and I couldn't mend it so that she could wear it on the street. But she will have a new pair soon. You see, last week was coal week, this week is rent week, and next week mother is sure she can get Luly's shoes, and then she can go to Sunday school again." And the princess smiled encouragingly.

Rosamond glanced at the shoes in question, and she thought she had never seen such a brave, pathetic-looking little pair. And their poor little owner had constantly to "tread careful," for Rosamond was sure that if she had given even the smallest skip they would have flown into pieces in spite of themselves.

Then Rosamond said delightedly, "I have a pair of shoes at home that will just fit Luly; I will send them this very afternoon."

You will be glad to know that she did so.

"But," continued she, "where is your mother?"

"Oh," explained the princess, "mother is away at work. You see, since father died she has to take his place and earn the living, and I take her place and keep the house and take care of the children."

"How many children are there?" asked Rosamond.

"Five," answered the princess brightly, "and they are such nice children, all of them, and they are learning so well in school. Why, it would surprise you the things they know."

"And you do the work for all this family," said Rosamond. "It is far too much for one so young and slight."

"I'm stronger than I look," said the princess cheerfully, "and I'm not young at all. I'm fifteen. Besides, the children are great helps, all of them."

Rosamond's heart gave a throb of pity as she glanced about the small, neat room, and she thought she had never known anyone quite so heroic in her life.

"Do tell me more about yourself," she begged.

But the princess did not know how to talk about herself. She told instead of her dear mother and how early she had to leave in the morning, how hard she worked, and how glad they were to see her come walking in at night. She showed the children's "Rewards of Merit" and their school exercises. She even unwrapped the baby's best dress from a clean towel and exhibited it. All her pleasure was to talk of the others. She had not a word for herself, although, as Rosamond saw, she was the very pulse of the machine, and that without her this happy home could never be at all.

And you may be sure that in that one visit Rosamond learned to love the brave, unselfish girl, and she was able to help her afterward in many ways.

This little story has no end. The princess still lives, and she is still keeping house and bringing up her little brothers and sisters. And she is a constant lesson, though she never dreams of such a thing, to all her friends, because she dignifies and makes beautiful the hard, monotonous labor of her daily life by her sweet, unselfish spirit, which is so like the spirit of the Lord and Savior whom she loves and of whose life she makes so true a copy.

⇥ FOR FURTHER THOUGHT ⇤

1. What is your job at home—something the whole family depends on you to do? What difference does attitude make when you're doing your assigned job?
2. Why do you think your mom and dad give you chores?
3. Describe the kind of girl who deserves the title of "princess."

To Working Girls

The time is never lost that is devoted to work.

EMERSON

Not slothful in business,
fervent in spirit,
serving the Lord.

THE BIBLE

IT IS A CONVICTION WHICH IS CONSTANTLY GROWING FIRMER among sensible people that girls should be educated to some business or profession as well as boys. I think this is a right view to take of the subject, for if we expect a young man after he has finished his school to put his shoulder to the wheel and do his share of the world's work bravely and faithfully, why should we not expect a young woman to do the same? Why is an idle young woman any more worthy of respect than an idle young man?

We have learned at last that in order to bring out the best that is in them, as well as to make them the happiest, we must train them to some congenial work. If they marry, they have the great benefit of the training and experience which honest work well done always brings; and if they do not marry, they are still content and happy in the knowledge that the thorough work which they are doing is of real use and service to the world.

"But," says Mabel, "do you think that every girl ought to leave home and go to work?"

"Not exactly," I answer, "for it is the clear duty of some girls to stay at home and 'help mother.'"

Where the mother is not very strong, or there is a family of young children to be brought up, it is to the elder sister that the mother must look for help, or life will become too hard for her and she will be forced to lay it down. Plainly, then, it is the daughter's duty when she has finished school life to devote her time and talents to her own home.

But a girl who does that is just as truly "in business" as if she were a bookkeeper or a dressmaker or anything else. And she earns her "allowance" just as much as if it were wages, as indeed it should be considered; and her friends should recognize that she is just as much self-supporting as if she went to work every morning and came home every Saturday night with her week's wages in her pocket. She is engaging in a business, and what is more, it is an excellent one, one which will render her independent if, as the years fly by, she should be compelled to earn her living among strangers; for a superior cook and an excellent housekeeper is always sure of a position at a good salary.

If a girl has an especial talent—and every girl has some peculiar gift, be it for writing, teaching, singing, mathematics, or anything else—let her remember that that talent was given her to use. The world has need of it, and if she does not cultivate it and make the most she can of it, she will be to blame.

"But," says Mabel, "do you think that rich girls—girls whose fathers can support them just as well as not—do you think they ought to work just the same as anyone else?"

To this I answer emphatically, "Yes." Money can never take the place of work. Every healthy woman ought to be capable of earning her own living. She ought to do it for the sake of the mental and moral discipline which it will be to her own nature, and she ought also to do it for the sake of others. If she is likely to have the management of money in future years, she certainly ought to have a good business training so that she may take care of it intelligently both for her own sake and for others; for no one has the right to use a fortune exclusively for one's self. Most of the inhabitants of this world are working people, and no one can understand their needs unless life has been looked at from a worker's point of view. Therefore a girl with money ought to be able to practically demonstrate that she can earn her own living, and then if it seems right for her to stop working for money and to devote herself entirely to others, she will be fitted by practical experience for that great task.

There is still another reason why a rich girl ought to know how to work: in this country where fortunes are made and lost so easily, how often do you hear it said of a rich man's daughter in the day of sudden calamity, "Poor girl! Now she will have to earn her own living. What *will* she do?"

There should be no more reason for such a remark to be made of a healthy young woman in the full possession of all her faculties than there is of a young man under the same circumstances, and we would scorn to speak with such commiseration of any young fellow.

So, my girls, whether you are rich or poor, find out what your particular bent is, then choose your work in life, and do it thoroughly and well as a servant of Christ; and then some day, when the time comes for you to leave this dear old world for a place that is still more beautiful, you will hear a gentle voice saying to you words which are well worth working for a lifetime to win, "Well done, good and faithful servant; enter thou into the joy of thy Lord."

⊰ FOR FURTHER THOUGHT ⊱

1. Why would it be a good thing to work, even if you had enough money that you didn't have to?

2. Who does a person really work for? (*Hint:* If you answered "self," go back and read the story.) How should that knowledge affect the way you view work?

3. After you finish school, if you could do anything you wanted to do, what would that be?

To Working Girls Again

I am glad that a task to me is given
To labor at day by day;
For it brings me health and strength and hope,
And I cheerfully learn to say,
Head, you may think; heart, you may feel;
But, hand, you shall work alway.

MISS ALCOTT

Go on "trying," my child;
God will give strength and courage,
and help you to fill each day
with words and deeds of love.

MISS ALCOTT'S MOTHER

THERE IS A LARGE CLASS OF GIRLS WHO HAVE NO CHANCE TO
choose the work which they can do best and which
they would most enjoy. They must take what they can
get, for to be "out of work" is the greatest misfortune
that can befall them.

Life to such girls is apt to be rather wearing and
monotonous. They often have to work harder than
they should, and sometimes they are not paid fair
wages. They do not have much chance for fun, and it
is not easy to go on day after day doing the same thing
over and over, with no change or apparent opportunity for advancement; and yet I know today of girls

who are living just that sort of a life and who are happy and are making a bright and beautiful thing of it.

Some people have an idea that some sorts of labor are more honorable than others; that it is more honorable, for instance, to paint a picture than it is to make a dress, or that a clerk behind a counter is a more respectable member of society than a household servant is. In the sight of God, and in the sight of good people also, this is not so. All labor is honorable, and whoever does good work is worthy of respect.

Then again, some people have an idea that there is work in the world that is easy to do, if it could only be found. That is also a mistake. Anyone who does thorough work of any kind has to work hard, and it is just as fatiguing to work with the brain as with the body, as those know who have tried both kinds of work. And having one's whole heart in one's work is a great incentive to feeling well, and the reward will be reaped in a less fatigued body and an easy mind.

Therefore, my girl who works, whatever your work may be, do it well. If your work seems hard and uncongenial, never mind. If there seems to be no chance of rising out of it to some more attractive place, still do it heartily just the same; because it is *right* for you so to do, and only so can you serve your Lord and Master.

Did you ever think how many years of His matchless life our Savior gave to hard manual labor? Do you suppose that there was no other occupation in all this world that the Lord of glory would have found more congenial to His nature than the one which He followed as boy and man for the best part of thirty years? "Jesus, the carpenter's son," they used to call Him there in Nazareth, and I never smell the sweet, fresh scent of newly sawed lumber, nor see the pretty, curling shavings as they drop from the plane, that I do not think of the long years of quiet work which He had there in that little country village. He had few congenial friends, I should imagine; people did not understand Him very well, and of the work which lay before Him He could not speak. He lived the quietest and most monotonous of lives; but, nevertheless, of one thing I am sure, that He was known throughout all the region as a good workman; and beside that, in His daily life He was so considerate and so friendly that there was no home where He was not welcomed gladly; and if anyone had either a joy or a sorrow, He always longed to share it with him.

Try, therefore, like Jesus to always do thorough work, and to do it in a cheerful spirit. It is surprising how much easier work becomes when it is done thus; and it is strange how such a spirit not only helps one's self, but every one around feels braver and better for living near any one who radiates such an atmosphere.

There is another reason for working well: good work in this world is a rarity. It is so rare that it is always noticed. No matter what you do, if you do it well it will surely attract attention, and it will be rewarded. So if you wish, as every girl should, to rise to a more responsible position, to earn more money, to have greater advantages, work well. You may not see the ghost of a chance to better yourself, but that is no matter; if you do your duty, God will provide the opportunity.

Then to working girls I would say: Take the very best care of your health that you can. Buy the most comfortable clothes that you can afford. Eat the most nourishing food that you can get. Take as much exercise in the open air as possible. Walk to the place where you are employed if you can, but give yourself a little bit of fresh air every day anyway; fifteen minutes' time spent out of doors on the porch or in the yard is better than nothing.

Then even a girl who works can get some chance to read, and it is surprising how much good a little reading does if one's heart is in it. You can read a little from your Bible every day, and I hope you always look over a good daily paper, and no girl's mind is entirely uncultivated who does these two things; and you can get a chance to read a book that is really worthwhile beside, if you take it a little at a time, I am sure, for I know many working girls who do. And if you will try, with Christ's help, to live this sort of a life, being gentle and brave and patient, you will be happy as well; and by-and-by you will have the sweetest surprise that can come to anyone, that of knowing that your heavenly Father is well pleased with you, and that you have by your true and beautiful earthly life been a help and comfort and inspiration to many.

⊰ FOR FURTHER THOUGHT ⊱

1. What does the author's advice reveal about girls years ago?
2. How are you like those girls? How are you different?
3. What part of the advice is timeless—what part can you apply to your life?

To Poor Girls

The journey of high honor lies not in smooth ways.
SIR PHILIP SIDNEY

One of the good things that accompany good blood
is that its possessor does not much mind a shabby coat.
GEORGE MACDONALD

THERE IS A TEACHER UNDER WHOSE SPECIAL TUITION OUR heavenly Father puts some of us while we are sometimes still very young, whose training produces—providing the scholar has a noble nature—the most admirable results. Few of us, I fear, would choose this teacher of our own accord, for she is very forbidding to look at and very stern in her method of training, and she gives long lessons usually, which are very hard to learn. Her name is Mistress Poverty; and it is a fact that there are no people in this world who are so brave, so noble, so true, and so loving as those who have been educated by her. It is true that there are some whom she fails to benefit, and they are the faint-hearted and the cowards who are not brave enough to learn the lessons she sets. Such people become bitter, sour, and unhappy, envious of those who are what they call "better off," blaming God for giving them what is really the most glorious opportunity of their lives. Such people are life's failures, and to have to live with one of them is the most disheartening thing I know of.

It is not easy, my child, to always have to go to school in a dress which is scant and shabby, instead of having a pretty and stylish suit, such as other girls have. It is not easy to have to wear cheap shoes with patches on them, instead of those pretty handmade dongola kid ones which you would like to have. It is not easy to have to clean your ribbons with benzine instead of buying new ones, or to have to wear the old coat which is too short for you, and that old felt hat again, when you thought you were surely done with them both last year. It is not easy for you never to be able to treat the other girls to caramels or ice cream. It is harder still for you to know that your dear father and mother have to strain every nerve to pay each quarter's tuition for you, and to feel that it is very uncertain whether you will ever be able to finish your course. These things are not easy. No. They are hard to meet aright. The girl who lives such a school-life as this with a sweet and patient courage, studying as if each term might be her last, is of the stuff of which heroes are made; and she will make a woman that will be so brave and sweet that only God and the good angels can estimate her worth or tell the good her life on earth will do. Such women are a help and inspiration so long as they live, and their memory is a joy for ever.

It was Ethel who said to me, "I never could be like that."

And I answered her plainly, "I know you can if you will; and if you are not worthy of the opportunity that is offered you, it will be your own fault."

You see, Ethel had a chance to go for four years to an excellent school. It was just what she needed to finish her education, but she hesitated about going because she knew she could not dress as well nor spend as much money as the other girls.

"The girls won't like me," said Ethel, half crying. "They will laugh at me and talk about me behind my back; I know they will."

"Would you despise a girl because she was poor?" I asked.

"You know I would not," answered Ethel.

"Then," said I, "do you think there are no other girls in this world who are as just and fair as you are? I assure you there are many girls in that school who will care no more about your clothes than they will about the color of your hair. If you are a good scholar they will respect you, and if you are pleasant and kind they will like you."

"But," insisted Ethel, "you cannot be recognized socially unless you have at least some money. Nice people will not recognize you unless you have nice clothes."

"You have made a mistake," said I. "That is merely a foolish fancy of yours. I have a dear and noble friend who, when she was a girl of seventeen, was obliged to leave the excellent school where she expected to finish her education for the purpose of earning her own living and assisting to support her family. If she could have had the opportunity to train herself for it, she had the mental capacity to obtain some intellectual occupation, which would have been congenial to her; but she had no time for that. She moved with her family to a distant city where they had no friends, and took a situation in a shop. Her employers soon discovered her worth and advanced her to a position of trust with a good salary. She was obliged, however, to devote the principal part of her earnings to her family, only reserving enough to dress herself in the most simple and inexpensive manner. She, with her family, united with a church near her residence and quietly began to attend its services, and little by little the pastor and people began to find them out and to learn what a valuable family they were. My friend had no time for society. Her working hours were very long, and in the evenings she was too fatigued to do anything more than to quietly rest in her rocking chair and then retire early so as to be ready for the duties of another day. Nevertheless, friends found her out, and they were among the most cultured and desirable members of the church, for it is such people who are the quickest to appreciate such heroism as this girl showed; and often one and another, when they were near her place of business, would run in to exchange a pleasant word and a cordial handshake across the counter with her.

"For five years she led this life, and for all that time I used to watch her lovely face in church, looking so brave and sweet, as her calm eyes were lifted to the minister's face in earnest attention while he preached. There were others watching her too, and one, a gentleman of wealth and position, succeeded in winning her for his own. And at last she stood in her snowy bridal robes by his side, beloved and honored, happy beyond words, surrounded by crowds of loving friends proud to testify their regard for her. And she was valued far more for the heroic and beautiful life which she had lived than she would have been under any other circumstances. In fact, it was just because of that life that her husband and all those friends had been drawn to her. Without it she never would have won the social position, the friendship, and the affection which are her reward."

So, my girls who are poor, do not fret or scold or turn bitter because of any lack of money. The things which money will buy are the least valuable things in this world, while the things which Mistress Poverty will teach you are beyond all price. Learn, therefore, with a good courage and a patient spirit, all the lessons which she sets you, rejoicing that your Lord and Master has counted you worthy of such heroic teaching.

⊰For Further Thought⊱

1. Name some people, places, and things that you're thankful for.
2. Why are you thankful for the people you mentioned? For the places? For the things?
3. Why is it a good thing to have to work for what you have?

On Courage and Self-Control

The bravest are the tenderest,
The loving are the daring.

Bayard Taylor

Courage and self-control are twin virtues every woman should possess, for she will surely need them sometime on her journey through life. And, as a rule, they are qualities which do not come naturally to either men or women. But I think that usually a man cultivates courage and self-control more than a woman does.

A man is ashamed to show fear; it is considered unmanly. But a woman will often confess to very foolish fears, and she will show fear sometimes when there is no real danger, and she is not at all ashamed of her cowardice. The reason of this dates back to childhood's days. If a little boy gets a bump on his forehead which makes him "see stars," he will instantly struggle to keep back the tears. His little face may be scarlet, his teeth clinched, and his mouth twisted with the effort not to cry, but every force of his nature will be exerted to keep his self-control, and he will be encouraged in his efforts. He is "papa's soldier," "papa's brave boy;" and there is nothing he dreads so much as being called a "coward" or a "cry-baby."

But if his sister gets a similar hurt, she is often encouraged to cry; it is considered no shame to her because she is a girl. As she grows older, when things go wrong either at home or at school, those ready tears spring again; and sometimes she sobs and cries until she is nervous and hysterical, and then she has to be soothed and petted and perhaps even the doctor has to be called to give her some quieting medicine before she can regain her composure. This is the kind of a girl who is apt to be afraid of the dark, afraid to be alone, afraid of ghosts, maybe, and she is afraid of mice and spiders and bugs and worms and all sorts of little harmless live creatures. She cannot bear to take a sliver from her brother's finger, she faints at the sight of blood, she is terrorstruck in a thunderstorm. All girls are not like this, but I have known such girls, have not you? I never feel like laughing at them; I am sorry for them; for though their fears may be silly, they are often real terrors to them, and when genuine trouble comes they are so undisciplined that they are quite unable to bear it.

It is difficult to get such girls to believe that they are responsible for their own behavior, that they could control themselves if they would. It will take time to learn the lesson, but it can be done. In the first place they must take care of their health, for very timid girls are never strong and hearty. How can they be with such quivering nerves and excitable imaginations? Plenty of out-of-doors for them, then, and good food and early hours. A healthy girl is naturally more composed and braver than a sickly one. And then, my "nervous" girl, resolve that you will control yourself under all circumstances. Do not cry for trifles. God gave tears to us to be our relief under hard trials. There are times when it is right to cry, but do not cry for nothing.

If you are haunted by any particular terror, set yourself to overcome it. Once I knew a young girl who was afraid of the dark. She said she could go into the dark well enough, but when she turned to go back toward the light it seemed to her that a dreadful pair of hands was reached out to clutch her, and she had to run with fluttering heart and panting breath back to light and safety. Foolish of course it was, but none the less dreadful to this small damsel. She set about curing herself, however. Every night on the stroke of nine she would leave the sitting room and go upstairs to the third story, in the dark all the way, and entering a certain long closet which was as dark as Egypt, she would touch a certain shelf in its farther corner, and then she would turn and walk slowly out and back to the light again. The first time she did so, as she turned the angle of the staircase her shadow jumped out before her, and she screamed. "What is the matter?" called her mother from below. "Nothing," she answered in a funny voice, as trembling but plucky she went on. In a few weeks her terror had vanished, and she was able to go about in the darkness as composedly as in the light.

There is still another way by which you can conquer any fear, and that is by trust in God. No one who absolutely trusts Him can ever be really afraid of anything. Should it be His will to take you to heaven by a stroke of lightning or by some great ocean storm, you can go as calmly as you would from your own little white bed in your own familiar room where you have slept since you were a baby, knowing that God will take just as good care of you in one place as in the other.

Every girl ought to have a knowledge of nursing

the sick, for even in these days of trained nurses it often happens that some dear one with a cheerful face and loving voice, if she has the requisite knowledge and skill, can win a patient back to health when no hired nurse could do it. And if death instead of life should be the result of the sickness, and you can have the courage to stand bravely and calmly by while the one you love passes through the "valley of the shadow," your presence will be a comfort unspeakable, and afterwards you will be always glad that you were able so to do.

Every girl ought to have a knowledge of simple surgery also. It is not often that an amateur has a chance to do anything great in the surgical way; but it matters a good deal to the children if mother or sister knows how to dress a cut, a bruise, or a burn comfortably. If you can take a course of lessons in "First Aid to the Injured," do so by all means, for it may be possible for you to save a life sometime, if you possess the knowledge and can apply it.

It is well to remember that a panic never made a bad matter better; and it is surprising how calm one can be during a frightful experience if one is only self-controlled.

A young lady whom I know was teaching out on a Western prairie, when glancing from a window she saw the vast funnel-shaped cloud of a cyclone sweeping toward the house. She had never seen one before, but she knew what it meant well enough, and she instantly gave her orders like the commander that she was: "John, shut the door, Harry and Ben, the windows. The rest remain seated." And she herself sat down in her chair.

The next moment the cyclone took up that schoolhouse, with sixty children and the teacher in it, moved it along the level prairie for a space of fifteen feet, and set it down right side up with care.

In a few minutes the door was hurriedly opened by two excited men who had from a distance witnessed the whole thing. They expected to find that the teacher had fainted, that the scholars were crazed with fright, and everything in confusion. What they did see was an orderly school, the teacher with a book in her hand, and the scholars about to recite.

"Don't you know what has happened?" stammered one of the astonished men.

"Oh yes," answered the teacher, "we have had a cyclone, but we are all quite safe."

"I declare!" said the would-be rescuer to his companion, "I don't believe she knows enough to be scared."

"I see no sense in being scared when the danger is all over and no harm has been done," observed Miss Vermont calmly. "Scholars, we will go on with the lesson."

They brought some ox-teams and hauled that girl's schoolhouse back to its original position, and she taught the children of that neighborhood for several years; and not the least valuable of the lessons which they learned of her was the one of coolness and composure which she taught them on the day of the cyclone.

It is a mistake to think that courage only belongs to those who have great physical strength. The bravest thing in life is a mother-dove. And the most delicate and sensitive women often show a courage and a self-control which are magnificent; and I hope every girl who reads this will resolve to cultivate these qualities, no matter how timid or how nervous she may be. She can succeed if she will try; and then, when she is a woman, how well her friends will love her and trust her. She will be their shield and comfort in the day of calamity, and no matter what she has to bear for herself or for others, she will be able to take it bravely, for God never fails to help those who put their trust in Him.

◄ FOR FURTHER THOUGHT ►

1. How do many girls react to scary things? How do many boys react? Why do you think there's a difference?
2. Can you think of a time when you were scared but you remained calm anyway? If you were with others, what effect did your calmness have on them?
3. What is a good way to overcome fear?

Weekday Holiness

She doeth little kindnesses
Which most leave undone or despise;
For naught which sets the heart at ease,
Or giveth happiness or peace,
Is low esteemed in her eyes.

Blessing she is, God made her so;
And deeds of week-day holiness
Fall from her noiseless as the snow;
Nor hath she ever chanced to know
That aught were easier than to bless.

Lowell

"Are you acquainted with your new neighbors yet?" I inquired of my friend Mrs. Fanshawe one bright morning, as we met going to market. Mrs. Fanshawe lived on the second floor of a pleasant apartment house, and a new family had rented the flat just above her.

"No," said she, "I have not called upon them yet, though I speak to one or two of the children. But I will tell you one thing," she went on in her enthusiastic way, "there is a girl in that family that I just love."

"What is she like?" I asked.

"I don't know," answered my friend, "I have never seen her, but she is lovely."

"I should like to know how you found that out," said I, "when you never have seen the young lady. I have heard of love at first sight, but love without any sight at all is a rarity."

My friend laughed. "I will tell you how I know," said she. "To begin with, there are in the family a father, a mother, a grandmother, and six children, and I think that my little love—her name is Bess—is the eldest of these, and the youngest child is a little fellow of four. They moved in very scientifically. The carpets were put down before anyone came, and just before the first load of furniture arrived Bess came. I could hear her voice distinctly telling the men where to put the things. It was a young voice, but with such a calm, sweet tone; she knew where everything was to go and nothing seemed to fluster her. Soon two young girls walked up the street, one carrying a clock and the other an old-fashioned Dresden china shepherd and shepherdess, and they were followed by a boy lugging two big baskets filled with family treasures. These children acted as the average child does. They ran about and pulled and hauled and tried to help, and sometimes disagreed a little, and then I would hear that lovely voice of Bessie's evidently settling matters, for presently all would be quiet again.

"By-and-by the mother and grandmother arrived in a carriage with the little fellow, and in a minute Bess was down at the door to help her grandmother up the stairs. By this time I was interested. I didn't exactly listen, you know, that is, I didn't eavesdrop; but whatever was plain to be seen and heard by any one I didn't think was any harm for me to know, and I began to want to know what Bess would do next. She was a good while in helping her grandmother upstairs, for the old lady is infirm, and her mother passed on ahead. 'I do hope,' said I to myself, 'that she will praise that child for the way she has managed.' I need not have been afraid, for she came to the door and I heard her say to Bess at the top of the stairs, 'Why, Bess, you have done wonders. The place really looks homelike!' Bess laughed, and they all went in and the door was shut.

"For the next three or four days the family were busy getting settled, and they could not one of them seem to do anything without Bess. It was 'Bess, Bess,' all day long, and I could hear her quick, light step going here and there as they called her, and then that voice of hers or her laugh—for she is a merry soul—a minute after. I felt sorry for her at first, she seemed to be so hard worked; but I am getting over that, for it is plain to be seen that her family appreciate her and try to take care of her.

"I heard her mother call to her from the kitchen, while I was at the elevator shaft, 'Bessie darling, go at once and lie down and rest yourself.'

"And when her father comes home at night he begins to run as soon as he reaches the second flight, and she runs also to open the door, and the first thing he says is, 'How is my Bess?'

"The other day, too, I met the third sister, Sara,

coming up the stairs with two pots of primroses, one under each arm. She and I speak, so I said, 'What lovely flowers!'

"'Yes,' she answered, looking delighted. 'They are for my sister Bess. She is so fond of them.' And as I went out of the door, there sat the little brother on the step, and he was polishing with his kilt some blue and yellow glass which he had found on the dust-heap. 'They are for my sister Bess,' he explained. 'You shut one eye, look through the glass with the other, and it changes the looks of the whole world. Would you like to try it?'

"I declined with thanks. 'Do you think your sister will like them?' said I dubiously.

"'Of course she will like them,' said he, with calm certainty. 'She will think them most surprising and beautiful.' He told me afterwards that 'Bess was delighted.'"

Not long afterwards Mrs. Fanshawe and I called on the new neighbors, and we saw this wonderful girl. She seemed timid and retiring, and did not take much part in the conversation. Nevertheless we learned in time that she was all that Mrs. Fanshawe had fancied and more. Said her grandmother once in speaking about her, "I never saw such a child. She is her grandmother's staff, her mother's right hand, her father's sunshine, and to her younger brothers and sisters she is more than lovely. I do not think she has ever lost her temper with one of them."

And I know that this was no idle praise: it was literally true.

"To know her is to love her," said one of her young friends to me. "And what a host of friends she has, hasn't she?"

"And," went on Edith reflectively, "although I think so much of her, I believe I have never yet found out exactly what her charm consists in. She is not pretty; she is not particularly gifted; and though she is intelligent, she has not had exceptional advantages for culture, and yet everybody is so enthusiastically fond of her."

"I think I know the charm," said I. "It is because she does not scorn to do little things; for, after all, it is the little things that make the comfort and happiness of our lives. It is folding her grandmother's shawl straight, it is making the mayonnaise dressing for the salad, it is building card-houses for Jack when he is cross, it is putting the flowers in Say's hair when she goes to a party, it is thanking the minister for a good sermon, it is saying, 'Lovely day, isn't it, Bridget!' when she goes into the kitchen; and she has such a hearty, sympathetic way with her, as if she was delighted to do anything for anybody, that everyone's heart goes out to her."

"I believe you are right," answered Edith; "but how does she keep it up year in and year out in the way she does? Does she never get tired and cross and nervous like common mortals?"

"Oh yes," I answered, "I am sure she does sometimes."

"Well," said Edith curiously, "how does she manage not to show it?"

"She has her refuge," said I, "and it is a very good place to hide in when one is tired and worried. She is everybody's friend, but her best Friend lives in heaven, and it is to Him she goes at such times."

"I know she is a Christian," answered Edith, "and one of the most consistent ones I ever knew; but somehow I had not thought of attributing her lovely ways to that; I thought they were altogether natural."

"I think they are the result of a deliberate cultivation," said I. "It is her idea of the way a Christian ought to behave."

"Well," said Edith gravely, "she is right about it, and I am sure she sets us all a beautiful example."

And I also agree with Edith, for I think that if every young girl would recognize her privileges, and should live in such a spirit, great good and blessing would come to thousands of homes.

⇥ FOR FURTHER THOUGHT ⇤

1. Which quality—talent, thoughtfulness, beauty, athletic ability—do you think gets the most attention over a long period of time?
2. Why do the little things we do for others make such a big impact?

—————◆•◆—————

"N. B."

We have left undone those things
which we ought to have done.

PRAYER BOOK

These ought ye to have done,
and not to leave the other undone.

JESUS

CARRIE MANNERING WAS A NICE GIRL. EVERY ONE WAS AGREED
about that. There was no more reliable girl in Mrs. Annersley's school. She always had done her lessons well, and
she had a perfect mark in conduct every day. At home
she was a good girl too. She did her share of the work,
she was always neat and tidy, she was up on time in the
morning, and she was as thorough and accurate and
steady as possible. There are not many girls who are equal
to Carrie; and yet there was a lack in Carrie's character,
and every one felt it. Her gentle, self-sacrificing mother
used to look at her sometimes with a sigh.

"Don't be so sharp with Jack, Carrie," she would
say, when Jack had left his muddy overboots on the
sitting-room rug or his wristlets on the card-receiver
in the hall.

"But, mother, he ought not to do such things,"
Carrie would answer.

"True," her mother would respond, "but perhaps

he will learn to be less careless by the time you have learned to be more patient."

Or it would be, "Oh, Carrie, could you not have run upstairs and brought Papa his umbrella! He is not at all well today."

"He did not ask me to, Mamma."

"But you should have noticed, my child."

You see, Carrie was so absorbed in her own life that she had very little time or thought for other people.

One morning as Carrie came into school a little group of girls were talking about her; she naturally paused as she heard her name mentioned. It was Milly Johns who was speaking.

"Oh yes," she was saying excitedly, "I know Carrie Mannering is a good girl, but I hate that kind of goodness. I would rather be bad than to be good like that. She makes me provoked with her superior airs; she thinks of nothing but herself and how she can get on and be better and better and better."

"I have heard every word you have said, Milly Johns," said Carrie, drawing nearer with her chin up, her eyes snapping, and her lip quivering with insulted pride.

"I don't care if you have," retorted Milly. "It is the truth I've been saying, and I hope it will do you good."

Carrie was very angry; but suddenly she remembered how only last Friday when they were doing dictation exercises she broke the point of her pencil, and this same Milly Johns passed her another at once, that she might not be obliged to stop and sharpen her own. She remembered too the friendly nod and smile with which Milly did this little deed. Milly was always doing such little things. She recalled also how the day before yesterday, as they were passing out of school, Milly had inquired of her wistfully, "Have you got that fourth example, Carrie?" Milly was not quick at figures. "Of course I have," Carrie had answered carelessly, and passed on.

Next day Milly missed that example, and Carrie reflected that a few words from her would have explained its principle to Milly and she could have been perfect too.

Still Carrie hardened her heart. "I do the best I can," she said stubbornly to herself, "and if everyone did as well, people would not need helping so much."

On Sunday the girls' teacher, Miss Sophie Willing, was talking to them about what she called "practical Christianity."

"How can you be sure that a girl is a Christian?" said she.

"When she belongs to the church," answered one.

"Not always," answered Miss Sophie gravely.

"By her character," said Carrie.

"What constitutes a Christian character?" continued Miss Sophie, questioning deeper.

"Well," answered Carrie slowly, "if you live just as nearly right as you can, do your work and your lessons well, and never do anything wrong, I think that comes pretty near to being a Christian."

"Right, Carrie," answered Miss Sophie, "it comes pretty near, but it is not the genuine thing. Do you not remember that young man who had kept all the commandments from his youth up, and yet he went away from Jesus sorrowful? What is your idea about it, Rose?"

"I think," said Rose gently, "that if a girl is truly a Christian she will be very kind and loving to everybody."

"Yes," said Miss Sophie, "if a girl is a true Christian she will be all that Carrie has described and more: she will have the lovingkindness which Rose speaks of added. As Christ has said, 'These ought ye to have done, and not to leave the other undone.'"

Now Carrie thought that Miss Sophie was talking right at her when she said this, and she was irritated at once.

"Well," said she, "I think that if every one did her duty in this world, she would not have to have so much done for her."

"That is very true, Carrie," said Miss Sophie, smiling, "but what would have become of this poor world if Jesus had talked like that when He was here?"

"But," said Carrie rather less hotly, "I don't have any time to do anything for other people, I am so busy with my own work; besides, I don't seem to have many chances to help others anyhow."

"We all know you are a busy girl, Carrie," answered Miss Sophie gently, "but still I am sure you have time to throw a crumb to a hungry sparrow or to pat the dog or to give a pleasant glance to a friend as you pass by. And surely you can find plenty of such little chances as that, and if you are quick to take them you can sweeten life for a great many in the course of a day."

Now Miss Sophie was in the habit of giving to each of her girls a little verse at parting, to help them through the coming week. Frequently it was from the Bible, sometimes it was a bit of poetry or some prose selection which she thought they would find helpful, and when Carrie opened her slip on the church steps that day she found written in it these two letters only, "N. B." What could that mean? Suddenly it flashed upon her that the letters stood for the Latin words *nota bene*, Mark well! Carrie smiled. It was just like Miss Sophie to do such a thing. She began to be ashamed of the irritation which she had shown in class. Then she remembered the remark of Miss Sophie's, "What would have become of this poor world if Christ had talked like that when He was here?"

How strange of Miss Sophie to contrast her foolish words with His loveliness, her miserable little life with His matchless one! She felt ashamed of her self-righteousness, ashamed through and through.

On reaching home she entered the sitting room where her mother was sitting, trying to write her Sunday letter to grandma, with Baby Bud fretting and teasing on the floor beside her, demanding her attention every minute.

"N. B.," said a voice in Carrie's ear. Now Carrie always got her lesson for next Sunday upon Sunday afternoon, and so had it off her mind for the coming week. "N. B.," said the little voice again clearly.

"Mamma," said Carrie, "I will take Bud upstairs and amuse her while you write."

"Will you, my dear?" said her mother with a relieved look. "I shall be so glad. But your Sunday school lesson?"

"I will get that another time," said Carrie cheerily, as she carried Bud away.

It was surprising how these two absurd little letters haunted Carrie all the week. When she came home from school on Monday she found her mother gone, the sitting room fire out, and Jack curled up on the sofa with a toothache. Now Carrie would have taken care of Jack in any case, but she had unusually long lessons to learn that day, and I am afraid if it had not been for the two letters she would have been impatient. But now she ran upstairs for laudanum and a little cotton, which she pressed into the hollow tooth; then she covered Jack snugly, built the fire, and then went back to the sufferer, and passing her hand through his rough hair gently, she said, "How is the pain now, Jackstraw? Better?"

There was something so gentle and sweet about her that Jack was surprised.

"It is a little better," said he. "Come and sit down by me, Carrie; you are almost as good as mother." So she took her books and sat by him till he was asleep.

So it went on all the week. Carrie was surprised to see how many chances she had of being kind when she took notice. She began to think she must have been a very selfish girl before. It did not interfere with her work or lessons either. True, it took a little planning and some self-sacrifice, but it paid every time.

Carrie did not stop trying when the week was over, for, as I said, she was a good girl and meant to do what was right. She kept on until her father and mother noticed the change and gave her loving looks and appreciative words.

Jack noticed it. "What's come over you, Carrie?" said he. "You are getting wonderfully nice."

Bud felt it. Twenty times a day she would put her little arms around Carrie's neck and say, "Dear Carrie, I love 'oo so!"

The girls at school saw it, and one day Milly Johns came to Carrie and said, "I am so sorry I spoke about you that way last term, Carrie. I think you are lovely."

"It was true then, Milly," said Carrie gravely, "but I hope I am not like that any more."

Finally one day Carrie told Miss Sophie about it, and this is what Miss Sophie put upon Carrie's slip of paper the Sunday after she had heard the story: "Inasmuch as ye have done it unto one of the least of these my brethren, ye have done it unto Me."

1. What one small thing did Carrie begin to do that changed the way people thought of her?
2. Name the character quality described in this story. (There may be more than one correct answer.)
3. Do an experiment this week. Use the initials N.B. (or make up initials or a word) to remind you to do little things for others. Put the reminder on Post-it notes where you can't miss them—the bathroom mirror, on your computer, in your notebook, in the refrigerator (don't tell anyone what it means, even if they ask!). At the end of the week, write a short description of what happened that week. Would you like to do it again?

"Born-to-vex-us"

That small, fretting fretfulness.

ANONYMOUS

The little rift within the lover's lute,
Or little pitted speck in garnered fruit
That, rotting slowly inward, moulders all.

TENNYSON

IT IS SUPERFLUOUS TO SAY THAT BORN-TO-VEX-US WAS NOT HER name. Her father dubbed her that once in a fit of exasperation, after a young lady whom Tennyson tells us about, and who was at one time a good deal of trouble to her father also. Her real name was Alice Thorne Ellsworth, and when her aunt Alice Thorne came to visit them, her niece and namesake was glad; for though she had not seen her aunt Alice since she was a baby, she was sure she would like her as soon as she looked at her; for Aunt Alice was an ideal aunt, young and pretty and gentle and bright, and with a trunk full of things which she brought home from Europe on purpose for her niece and her nephew.

"Now," said Ally to herself, "Aunt Alice will appreciate me; she will see how Papa laughs at me and Tom teases me and Mamma misunderstands me. I am sure she will see how it is, and I shall have a friend at last."

The first morning after Aunt Alice's arrival she came down to breakfast looking cheerful and bright. She gave Ally a kiss and Tom a small pinch on the ear, and she began to make them guess what she had brought them from Europe, and they were presently wrought up to such a height of expectation that Ally forgot to put on her usual expression; and for several days Aunt Alice's own cheerful ways were so infectious, and everyone was full of such delightful talk, and so many beautiful plans were proposed, that Ally forgot her usual woes and acted, as Tom said, "quite like other girls." And Papa privately inquired of Mamma where Born-to-vex-us had gone to.

But one rainy morning she appeared. The minute

Ally came into the room Tom saw that she wore what he called her "early Christian martyr" expression.

"What's the matter, Ladybird?" asked Aunt Alice.

"Isn't it *mean* that it rains so?" said the Ladybird in an injured manner.

"Why, no," responded Aunt Alice. "This rain is greatly needed, I am sure."

"I don't care," went on Ally. "I didn't want it to rain today a bit."

Aunt Alice eyed her niece observantly.

"Have some oatmeal," she said in a cheerful tone.

"No, thank you," responded Ally discontentedly. "Mamma," she went on, "I think this is a horrid breakfast. I am so tired of chops that I don't know what to do."

"Ally," said her father, "stop fretting and eat your breakfast quietly, if you have nothing pleasant to say."

After this Ally maintained an injured silence. Her mother looked pained, her father was evidently annoyed, and Tom quietly inquired at what hour she expected to be thrown to the lions.

After breakfast Ally had the parlors to dust and her own room to put in order, and there, after an hour or so, her Aunt Alice found her.

"What is the matter, little girl?" said she, pausing in the doorway. "Have you a headache?"

"Not exactly," answered Ally, sighing.

"Pain anywhere?" continued Aunt Alice.

"No, but I feel so miserable."

"You look as though you did," admitted Aunt Alice, as she vanished.

Later Mamma came hastily into the sitting room with a handful of white linen in her hand.

"Here are these four napkins," said she, looking at Ally doubtfully. "They ought to be hemmed, so as to go into the wash on Monday."

"I was just going to practice," said Ally gloomily, "but I'll hem them for you, Mamma."

"I wish you would," answered Mamma, "for really I haven't the time. Cut them by a thread and hem them neatly, for they are handsome material," and she went away again.

"It is always the way," said Ally. "If I want to do anything, Mamma is sure to want me to do something else." She settled herself in a low rocker and began her work.

"I would rather do anything than hem napkins," she presently complained; "they are so stiff."

At last they were done and she took them to her mother. "There," said she, "they are finished at last, and I have just about broken my back over them, and pricked my finger till it bleeds besides."

"Mamma never noticed whether the napkins were nicely done or not," she complained as she went back to her aunt Alice. "She just said, 'Very well, dear, put them in the hamper,' and went right on with what she was doing."

"What was she doing?" inquired Aunt Alice.

"Well," hesitated Ally, "she is trying to get my new dress done so I can wear it to church tomorrow."

"And did you thank her for all the dainty stitches that she is taking for you?" asked Aunt Alice, "and for all the thought and care which she is putting upon that dress that it may please and become you?"

Ally did not answer, but I am sorry to say that she flung herself out of the doorway in a fret, and ran up to her own room and had what she called a "good cry," and by-and-by she came downstairs acting more injured and distressed than ever.

That night after Ally had gone to bed, her father said with a smile and a sigh, "Well, Mamma, Born-to-vex-us has come back again, hasn't she? I was really in hopes Alice had exorcised her, but it seems not."

"Poor child!" sighed Mamma, "she has a very unhappy disposition."

"Is she often this way?" asked Aunt Alice.

"Yes," answered her mother, "I am sorry to say that she is, and the whole family dread the mood so much that we will do anything rather than bring it on; but it grows more frequent every year."

"Have you tried giving her a plain talk on the subject?" said Aunt Alice.

"Oh yes," answered Papa, "I have given her more than one."

"How does she take them?"

"Weeps," answered Papa laconically.

"Well," said Aunt Alice, "you cannot let her grow

up like that. May I try my influence with her?"

"I shall be only too glad to have you," replied Mamma, and there the subject was dropped.

A few days after Alice noticed that her aunt made an entry every now and then in a little notebook. But knowing that she was preparing for a shopping expedition, she did not think it strange. But when evening came, Aunt Alice took Ally up into her own room, and then she showed her what she had written. It was a list of every complaining and fretful word Ally had spoken during the day. She had said "Oh dear!" fifteen times. Eleven times things had been "horrid"; seven times they were "mean"; and Tom had been "hateful" every time he came into the house that day. Mamma had been very "unkind" three times, and Papa had "scolded" twice, while Bridget had been "impertinent" once. Ally had done seven things that she "couldn't bear" to do. She had had one "frightful" pain and one "dreadful" one. She had "despised" her music teacher. She had cried "because her new dress was not as pretty as Alice Cary's," and she had wished for five things which she did not possess, and had fretted because she could not have them.

"Now, Ally," said Aunt Alice, "this is an accurate account of your behavior for one day, and it is just an average day—no worse than many others and better than some. Take it and look at it and think it over." And without one more word Aunt Alice left the room.

This list was a very hard blow to Ally. There were

her faults spread out in black and white, and she could neither deny them nor excuse them. She cried, of course, but no tears could wash away that awful list.

The family said nothing, but they watched Ally very closely during the following week, and they saw that she was really trying to be pleasant and unselfish; but it was a great task, and it will take many a hard struggle before Ally can conquer this evil habit. But all her friends are trying to help her, and, best of all, she has learned to call upon a heavenly Friend for aid; and since she has turned to Him, I am sure she will win the victory over self at last.

⊰ For Further Thought ⊱

1. Why did Ally's father call her "Born-to-vex-us"? (Vex means "to bother.")
2. Ally needed to work on her habit of complaining and being in a bad mood. Why was Aunt Alice's list a good way to help Ally change?
3. What kind of list would Aunt Alice make about you if she could follow you around for a day?

Daydreams

Rise from your dreams of the future —
Of gaining some hard-fought field,
Of storming some airy fortress,
Of bidding some giant yield:
Your future has deeds of glory,
Of honor; God grant it may!
But your arm will never be stronger,
Or the need so great as today.

Adelaide Procter

Once there was a little house, and in it lived a father who was not very rich, a mother who was not very well, four jolly little brothers who were just as bright and active and full of fun as four small boys could be; and they had an elder sister named Maggie. Maggie was tall and slender and pretty; she had dark eyes and a good deal of black hair and she was of a very romantic disposition. She did not think life was worth living at all if one could not have a fine house to live in, beautiful clothes to wear, and plenty of compliments and admiration from rich and distinguished people. Because she felt like this, her own little home with its shabby furniture seemed hateful to her, the simple food which they had to eat unappetizing, the plain clothes which she wore a dreadful trial. Her little brothers she thought were very rude and rough, her father unkind, and her mother unsympathetic. And so, to solace herself for this hard state of things, she took to daydreaming.

She used to steal away from her mother and the little lads and go out in the quiet summer woods, and there she would seat herself in a picturesque attitude on some old log and dream the long golden hours away. She soon created for herself an ideal world quite different from anything which is known upon this humdrum planet, and there she lived, the heroine of her own romance.

"If I were rich," she used to say to herself, "I would very soon change things for us all. Papa and Mamma would learn how they misunderstand me when they call me selfish, for I would build them a beautiful home and fill it with all sorts of beautiful things. There should be pictures and statuary and rich silken hangings and the most elegant furniture. Mamma should always wear silk, and she should have crowds of servants to do her bidding; and I would build a special library for Papa, and every book in it should be beautifully illustrated and bound in Turkey morocco. Papa should be beautifully dressed too. He should have a fur-lined overcoat and a silk hat and a gold watch and gold spectacles and everything. The boys should wear black velvet suits and silk stockings all the time; and I would have plenty of tutors and governesses to take care of them, so that they never should come tagging after me or bother me at all. And as for me, I would have the most beautiful clothes in all the world. I would never wear anything but delicate pink or cream color, and all my gowns should be embroidered with silver and gold; and I would have the most magnificent jewels in the world as well. But I would be very generous with my money: I would not keep it all for myself as some rich people do. I would build grand churches and I would endow hospitals, and every one would admire me and love me, and they would call me 'Princess Margaret.' I would have suitors too, handsome gentlemen; but I would be very hard to win, and crowds would be happy if I just smiled once at them."

Here perhaps Jack or Ted would discover her hiding place, and call out, "Mamma wants you, Maggie, right away." And then this beautiful vision would burst like a bubble, and poor Maggie would come back to actual life again, and I do not wonder that it all seemed very poor and plain to her after her gorgeous dreams.

She would return to the house and her mother would say, "Daughter, where have you been so long? My head aches, and I must lie down while you get the tea; and see, the floor is still unswept because I was unable to do it, and the children need clean hands and faces before Papa comes home."

Then Maggie, with a frown between her eyes and a pettish curve to her pretty mouth—making an expression quite unlike that of the gracious Princess Margaret of her dream—would seize the broom and begin her tasks; but the work was never thoroughly done. The corners were unswept, the tablecloth was put on askew, and the dishes were put on anyhow, making anything but a cheerful meal for her tired father when he came in. And little Harry would often cry and say, "Sister Maggie is cross to me," because she rubbed his little face too roughly with the towel.

Of course Maggie's parents often felt anxious and grieved about her selfish and unlovely ways. Sometimes they reproved her, but that seemed to do no good; she only cried and said they did not love her, and acted more injured than ever.

She did not learn her lessons in school and her teacher could not make her apply herself, and no one knew what to do with her. She thought people were unjust and unkind to her; she looked upon herself as a martyr and dreamed her gorgeous daydreams more than ever.

Finally a new Sunday school teacher took the class of which Maggie was a member. She was a wealthy and beautiful young lady, and she was as good as she was beautiful. She attracted Maggie at once, for she was almost the ideal of some of Maggie's fairy tale visions.

As for the young lady—Miss Constance was her name—she looked at poor Maggie's cross, sour little face and wondered what could ail the child's spirit to make her appear so unlovely. She resolved to help her if she could, so she had her at her own home a good deal and did all she could to win her confidence and affection.

As Maggie became acquainted with Miss Constance

she found that hers was not at all the life she had imagined so rich a young lady would lead. It was not a life of ease and pleasure; she was busy all the time. She was her father's secretary, her mother's assistant about the house. She helped her younger brothers and sisters with their lessons and spent a good deal of time in the room of an invalid aunt. The whole family loved her and were proud of her and declared that they "could not live without her."

When Maggie saw all this she began to wish that she could learn to be like sweet Miss Constance, and after a while she opened her foolish little heart and told this kind friend all her troubles. Miss Constance did not smile at any of the absurdities, but when she had heard it all she gave to Maggie at once the gentlest and the plainest talk that Maggie had ever heard about herself in all her life.

Maggie could not be angry, for Miss Constance was too kind and sympathetic with her for that, though she showed her plainly how selfish and how foolish she had been.

"Very few girls have the opportunity to lead so noble a life as you have," said she to Maggie. "You can be your brothers' veritable good angel, if you will, and they will love you and trust you and be so proud of you. They will think there is nobody like you in a very short time, if you will only be kind and gentle with them. You can help to make them brave and noble men, and then some day it will be your turn to be proud of them. You can be such a comfort and joy to your good father and mother, if you will. Why, you can be a princess in disguise to the whole family, and you will be so happy."

Maggie smiled faintly, but when she went home that afternoon she resolved to try Miss Constance's plan. She did try and she persevered. It was hard work, she made many mistakes, but she struggled on. After a time she heard little Harry say to Ted, "I think Maggie is nicer than she used to be, don't you?"

"Yes," answered Ted, "and she is prettier too."

This pleased her, for she knew she was on the right track.

Her mother soon noticed the change in her ways, and told her she was getting to be a "real comfort." And one day her father brought home to her a pretty new gown, and as he gave it to her he said with a kiss, "I am so glad I can give it to my good girl!" and this made her happy indeed.

All this was long ago. Maggie is now a woman grown. She keeps the house for her father, for her mother went home to heaven some years since, and she is a great comfort and happiness to him. Her brothers are fine, well-grown young men, and she is very proud of them, while they think that Maggie is just about the loveliest woman in the world. And Maggie is far better and happier living so than she would have been if any of the wonderful dreams of her childhood had come true.

❧ For Further Thought ❧

1. In what style does the author tell this story? (*Hint:* F _ _ _ _ T _ _ _ .) Why do you think she used this style to talk about daydreaming?
2. Is there good advice for you in this story? How could you obey it?

On Manners

She who nips off the end of a brittle courtesy,
as one breaks off the tip of an icicle, to bestow on those
whom she ought cordially and kindly to recognize,
proclaims the fact that she comes
not merely of low blood,
but of bad blood.

Dr. Holmes

Courtesy is said to be love in little things,
and the one secret of politeness is to love.

Professor Drummond

A gracious manner is the greatest charm which a woman can possess. It is far beyond beauty or intelligence or wit. Without it the most gifted woman is unattractive, but with it a plain woman can be lovely.

Every girl admires the grace of beautiful ways, and most girls try in one way or another to cultivate them.

The girls who try the hardest sometimes fail, while those who do not seem to try at all are often charming. This makes some people say that good manners are a gift, but I think that is a mistaken idea.

I know a young lady who is anxious to make a good impression in society, and she has very nice manners indeed, which she is apt to take out with her best gloves and her party fan. She is deferential to elderly people, friendly with young people, and she knows the latest social ways of the hour, but she does not "get on" as she would like to do. Said a young man once, speaking of her, "She is very pretty, and all that; I never saw her do a thing or say a word that I could criticize: but, all the same, I don't like her."

Poor Molly makes many acquaintances, but she wins no friends. She is not a social success.

I know another girl, a little country girl, perfectly unused to city life, who was invited to spend a winter with some city cousins. Her face was not so pretty as Molly's, or her clothes nearly so stylish, but nevertheless, in her innocent way she was a genuine belle. Everybody went about saying, "Have you seen that little cousin of the Apthorps'? Isn't she lovely!" And all of the Apthorps' friends took her up and showed her about with the greatest kindness.

What was the difference between the two girls? Why was everybody so enthusiastic about the one and so indifferent to the other? The secret was simple: one never thought of herself, the other thought of no one else. One was constantly endeavoring to "make a good impression;" the other was always trying to show her friends how much she appreciated their kindness and loved them for it.

Sometimes you meet people who appear to keep the good manners for their intimate friends only. They act as if they had such a scant supply that they could not afford to waste any upon strangers. Marion is one of these.

"I don't see the use," she observed to me one day, "in being so polite to people whom you don't care for. I would do anything for a friend, but somehow I never can get on with people whom I don't take to, and I won't try. Some people like everybody. There is Jennie Livingstone now. She is good friends with quantities of people; but I care for only a few." And Marion looked as if she thought her exclusive nature was somehow superior to Jennie's bountiful one.

"I am sorry for you, Marion," said I. "I think you miss a great deal of happiness by acting like that."

"Well," she answered complacently, "I was made so, and it is no use trying to change one's nature."

"You are wrong there," I answered. "Anyone can cure a fault, whether it is one of nature or of training, if she will try."

"Oh, a fault!" exclaimed Marion, in surprise.

"Yes," I answered gravely. "Did it never occur to you that it is a fault for you to treat people whom you do not fancy so coldly and indifferently as you do? Do you not know that it is a sin to be rude?"

"I don't mean to be rude," said Marion.

"No," said I, "you only mean to be 'stiff' and 'formal' and 'chillingly polite' when you are not attracted by people, and there is nothing that hurts worse than to be treated like that. You have no right to hurt people's feelings. You ought to be kind to everybody."

"But," said Marion, "I can't endure slow people and stupid people. One can't like everybody."

"Christ did," I answered. "He loved the whole world. And when He was on earth He was very kind to people whom you would call both slow and stupid. Marion," I went on, "I think you have charming manners when you choose to use them, but you keep them for a very few people. You are making a mistake. You ought to use those pretty manners every day and keep your stiff ones for very rare occasions. You ought to use them with the seamstress and the postman, with your own family and with your schoolmates and teachers, and indeed with everyone whom you may meet during the day; and if you do this you will be surprised to find how many lovely natures there are among the lowly as well as among the high in this world, and how much goodness is hidden under unattractive exteriors; for beautiful manners are like a branch of witch hazel [a North American shrub], which discovers hidden springs, fresh and sparkling, of whose existence no one ever guessed before.

"You will find it easier to like people if you are

courteous to them, for they will like you and will turn their best side toward you always. You will have greater opportunities to be kind to people also, for when people love you and trust you, you can help them better than you possibly could otherwise."

"Oh dear," said Marion, "I never thought of it all in this way before."

"Did you never think," said I, "of what beautiful manners Christ had? In a few minutes He could make friends with a total stranger. What a charm His recorded conversations have! How courteous His greetings and His parting words were! If we try to copy Him at all we should certainly try to copy His manners, for they are not among the least of the beautiful examples which He sets us."

Now the root of a perfect manner is love. If you have a heart full of love you never can be rude, for you will not wish to hurt people's feelings; you will wish to please people, to help and to comfort them and to make them happier, and so your loving heart will prompt you to pay little deferences and respects where they are due. You will be quick to give the appreciative word and the sunny smile. Your manner will be interested, those small kindnesses called courtesies will be unfailing. And if you have a heart like this such manners will come easy to you, because they will become the habit of your life, and then, no matter in what company you may be—whether you are invited to dine with the queen or you go to take tea with your old nurse who took care of you when you were a baby—you will be equally at your ease, for when one has a heart that is full of the Spirit of Christ, one cannot do much that is amiss.

⊰ FOR FURTHER THOUGHT ⊱

1. How are good manners more than saying "Please" and "Thank you"?
2. What is the basic problem with a person who is polite only to get ahead or to impress people?
3. Describe the kind of person who is naturally good-mannered.

On Having Good Times

Not enjoyment, and not sorrow,
Is our destined end or way,
But to act, that each to-morrow
Find us farther than to-day.

LONGFELLOW

IT IS NOT ONLY NATURAL FOR YOUNG PEOPLE TO WANT TO HAVE good times in this world, but they ought to want them.

What would you think of a kitten that was so serious-minded that it did not want to chase its own tail? It would not be a very attractive kitten to me.

And a young girl who did not like candy or a pretty

gown, who did not care for tennis or to go skating, or like to be in charades or tableaux [a game like group solitaire], who could not talk nonsense or take a joke, and who did not like a genuine frolic of any kind — such a girl would be a poor specimen of girlhood to my mind, and I should not know what to do with her. But there are some girls who live for nothing but "a good time"; all the rest of life to them is merely incidental. The Bible says a very serious thing about such girls. It says, "She that giveth herself to pleasure is dead while she liveth." Notice it does not say she who likes pleasure, but she who *lives* for it; she is the one who is dead while she liveth. And what the Bible says is true. Did you ever watch a girl who lives for nothing but her own pleasure, and see how barren her life is of everything that is noble and unselfish and Christ-like? As for being happy, she does not know the meaning of the word. There is always something the matter with her "good times." The weather interferes with them. Her gowns do not suit her. The party is not lively enough. Somebody slights her. The music is not so sweet as she thought it would be. She is fretted, her feelings are hurt, and she is never satisfied. Poor unhappy child! All her thoughts center upon her miserable self, and she thinks of nothing but how she can best divert her poor selfish heart, which never is contented, and never will be while she lives like this.

But a girl who lives to do her duty bravely and sweetly as God shows it to her day by day, can take any good time which comes to her fairly and enjoy it with a zest.

Young people sometimes have a singular idea that religion and fun do not go together. They seem to think that once you become a Christian you must leave all your good times behind you; I do not know where that idea first originated. Sometimes I think it dates back to the period of the Roundheads [so named because of cutting their hair short in contrast to their political opponents, the Cavaliers, who wore their hair long], for those old Puritans seemed to hold the opinion that a solemn face was better than a sunny one, and that tears were more meritorious than laughter. They were noble souls, but in that they were mistaken. Such an idea is not to be found in the Bible from cover to cover, for the Bible expressly says "there is a time to laugh," and makes cheerfulness a Christian duty.

"But," says some thoughtful girl, "all amusements are not harmless; and how shall I know which is right and which is wrong?"

There is no inflexible rule about this, but there is a very simple way by which any conscientious girl can obtain an answer to that question. If you think Christ would approve, take the pleasure and enjoy it heartily. If you are in any doubt as to what He would wish, pass the pleasure cheerfully by.

The loveliest thing of all about good times is that they can be shared with others, and I think there is no sweeter way of serving God than this. True, at first it does not seem always easy. When you do have a good time you are apt to want only your own friends in it—people whom you know and like and are used to; it seems pleasanter so. But if, while you do not neglect your own friends, you let others join you also, you will find that you have better times than ever, for an unselfish act always brings its own reward.

Then there is another point to consider: there is no surer way to get a good influence over people than to let them share your pleasures. That new girl, for instance, who has just come to your school: she is rather shy and awkward perhaps; she does not look very interesting. Do not think you have done your duty by that girl when you have asked her to Sunday school and Christian Endeavor. Probably she will not accept such a formal invitation. But if you will also ask her to play tennis and to lunch with the other girls on some Saturday, she will believe in you and love you and will go with you anywhere you like.

Then did you ever think that there are people in this world—and some of them are young girls too—who never have any good times of their own? They have to work hard, and they know what it is to have constant care and anxiety. Sometimes they catch glimpses of you, my happy girls, flitting along in your pretty clothes. They see your smiling faces now and then, they hear the cheerful ring of your voices as you pass by, and that is all they know about good times. Think of them, and let them come within the charmed circle too, and give them a little taste of lighthearted happiness, to let them know you love them and sympathize with them.

I think God often teaches us by joy as well as sorrow, by pleasure as well as pain; and if we receive our good times unselfishly and thankfully as coming from His hand, we never need be afraid to take them, for we shall be nobler and better for every one which we enjoy.

⊰ FOR FURTHER THOUGHT ⊱

1. What does the Bible say about laughter (read Proverbs 15:13,15,30; 17:22)?
2. The author says, "There is no surer way to get a good influence over people than to let them share your pleasures." What does that mean?
3. Next time you and your close friends get together, invite someone from school or church to join you. After everyone goes home, read this story again and describe how "an unselfish act reaps its own reward."

On Growth

Build thee more stately mansions, O my soul,
While the swift seasons roll;
Leave thy low-vaulted past;
Let each new temple, nobler than the last,
Shut thee from heaven with a dome more vast,
Till thou at length art free,
Leaving thine outgrown shell by life's unresting sea.

DR. HOLMES

And Jesus increased in wisdom and in stature
and in favor with God and man.

THE BIBLE

THE MOST DELIGHTFUL OCCUPATION IN THE WORLD IS TO watch things grow. I do not care what, a flower, a kitten, a baby — anything that is alive and growing vigorously is a joy to see. But stop a minute; there is just one thing more delightful than seeing things grow; it is to *help* them grow. We cannot *make* anything grow, but we can help or hinder things a good deal, just as we choose.

This is worth thinking about for a little. How would you help a violet, for instance, to grow? You would give it the proper soil for violets. You would give it just enough water and plenty of air and sunlight, and you would keep all ills and harms away. As surely as you did this the violet would do its part. It would obey the law of its nature and take from the soil, the sunshine, and the air the things it needs to nourish it, and by-and-by the wonderful transformation would be wrought and you would have your blossoms for bouquet or vase.

So with the baby. We give her proper food and clothing, see that she gets her quiet sleep and plenty of fresh air, and plenty of love and cherishing and all the things that we know are best for babies, and her body, obeying the same law that governed the violet, is nourished. A wonderful change is constantly taking place in her curling hair, her round, rosy cheeks, her little pink nails, in every bone and muscle and nerve, and indeed down to the minutest part of her vigorous little body. The baby does not know it, but she *grows*, and we are glad.

Now it is just as easy for the soul to grow into a healthy and beautiful life as it is for the body, if we can but find out what things will nourish it best and use them.

When we see a particularly thrifty plant we say to the gardener, "How did you manage that plant to help it grow so finely?"

He tells us, and if we have a similar plant at home and follow his directions, in course of time our plant will be as beautiful as his. Now there never was any one in this world who had so beautiful a youth as Christ's, and I think if we could but find out how He was able to win that perfect character while He was still so young, it would be easier for us to grow like Him.

Perhaps you think we do not know very much about what sort of a boy Jesus was. I think we know a good deal. True, the Bible does not say much about His boyhood, but every word it does say counts. I know He was a well-grown lad, for one thing, healthy and strong, because He "increased in stature." I know He studied well and that He was observant and thoughtful, because He "increased in wisdom." I know He was an unselfish boy and hearty and genuine, and I am sure He was *pleasant*. I know this was so, because *everybody* liked Him—not just His father and mother and a few appreciative friends, but everyone who knew Him was drawn to Him. The Bible makes no exceptions. He was "in favor" with everybody. He was "in favor" with God also. So you can see how conscientious and upright and sincere He must have been.

Now how was it, do you suppose, that while He was still so young He built up such a beautiful character as this? Perhaps you think, because He was the Son of God, that He had no temptation to do wrong. But when He laid His Godhood by, He took our human nature upon Him, and the Bible says that He was tempted in all things just as we are, yet He was "without sin." How did He do it then?

I think He did it all by the beautiful grace of obedience. When He was a lad of twelve He minded His parents; He was "subject unto them." And indeed His whole life, down to the very hour of His death, was a beautiful example of perfect obedience.

Now this grace of obedience is a wonderful thing. It reaches throughout the whole realm of nature. The violet unconsciously obeyed a law of God when it added cell to cell throughout its system, until at last the perfect flower came. The little child does the same and grows likewise. And we who are older, if we obey the laws which God has given for our souls' health, will grow as well. We cannot help it.

There is another lovely thing about obedience; an obedient child is well beloved. There is nothing so touching to a father's or a mother's heart as a child who gladly obeys. So it is with our heavenly Father. He loves us to obey Him, and that makes it very sweet and easy for us to be obedient.

The process of growing is a quiet thing; we do not notice it ourselves. If we try to copy Christ we are very busy people. We have quantities of things to do both for ourselves and others. We cultivate ourselves that we may teach others; we control ourselves that we may help others; we are lighthearted that we may cheer them; we are brave, we are gentle, we are industrious, we are sympathetic for others. We resist temptation lest we should drag others down. We see what an intricate network our social life is: how we depend on each other and are influenced by each other; how no one can be good without helping someone else to be better, or be bad without injuring someone. The thought both frightens and inspires us, and we "go on trying," as the children say, harder than ever. This is just the way God meant we should live to let our own souls grow.

Are these thoughts too great and serious for a girl of sixteen to have—a pleasant, natural, hearty sort of girl? I do not think so. I know more than one girl of sixteen who not only thinks of these things, but lives this sort of a life; and everybody loves them and they love everybody, and they are the happiest kind of girls.

And now, my girl whom I do not know and yet of whom I am thinking—you whose eyes are passing along the last pages of this little book— if you have not already begun this sort of life, shouldn't you commence now?

If you try all by yourself you will find it very hard work, for your soul can no more thrive and bring forth flower and fruit without your heavenly Father's help than a violet can blossom in a cellar. But with God's help you will find it the most natural thing in the world, for all things are possible through Him who loved us and gave Himself for us, that we might be made perfect in Christ Jesus.

⊰ FOR FURTHER THOUGHT ⊱

1. What is the secret ingredient that helps us grow in the way God wants us to? (*Hint:* O_ _ _ _ _ _ _ _)

2. Many people will tell you to live for yourself— "You've got to take care of yourself because no one

else will." How is this advice contrary to what God tells us?

3. Why does God put us into relationships with people—our families, our friends, our schoolmates? What can we learn? What does He want us to practice? (*Hint:* L _ _ e)

There's more to teaching your kids about sex than a nervous discussion of the birds and the bees.

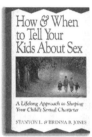

Our children are inundated with messages about sex. Everywhere they turn—in our neighborhoods, school, and the media—they are bombarded with discussions, jokes, debate, and mixed messages about sex. So how can we make our input count?

Stan and Brenna Jones suggest that sex education is not so much about information as it is about character formation. How our children act when it comes to sex isn't a matter of information, Bible verses, or warnings. It's about who they are.

How & When to Tell Your Kids About Sex will help you move beyond the "sweaty hands" approach to telling your kids about sex and give you the tools you need for building Christian character in your children that will equip them to take a stand and make the right choices.

How & When to Tell Your Kids About Sex: *A Lifelong Approach to Shaping Your Child's Sexual Character* (Stanton L. & Brenna B. Jones) 0-89109-751-1/$18

Available at your local bookstore or call (800) 366-7788 to order.